ISRAEL'S ENEMIES
WITHIN

ISRAEL'S ENEMIES
WITHIN

By
Shaul Katzav

Israel's Enemies Within by Shaul Katzav
Copyright © 2023 by Shaul Katzav
All Rights Reserved.
ISBN: 978-1-59755-698-9

Published by: ADVANTAGE BOOKS™, Longwood, FL
                       www.advbookstore.com

All Rights Reserved. No portion of this book may be reproduced in any form without written permission from the publisher or author, except as permitted by U.S. copyright law.

Library of Congress Catalog Number: 2023949099

Name:	Katzav, Shaul, Author
Title:	***Israel's Enemies Within***
	Shaul Katzav
	Advantage Books, 2023
Identifiers:	ISBN Paperback: 978159756989
Subjects:	Israel & Palestine
	Middle Eastern Politics

First Printing: November 2023
23 24 25 26 27 28   10 9 8 7 6 5 4 3 2 1

CONTENTS

Chapter 1 **Israel's Enemies Within** 1

Chapter 2 **Trojan Horses in the Israeli Knesset** 9

Chapter 3 **Thank God the Bible Was Not Written by Religious People** ... 27

Chapter 4 **On the Way Back Home** 39

Chapter 5 **Red vs Blue-and-White Zionism** 51

Chapter 6 **"Sons of Shem"** 63

Chapter 7 **The Tyranny of the Israeli Supreme Court** 71

Chapter 8 **The Few Affecting the Many** 81

Preface to Chapter 9 91

Chapter 9 **The Final Chapter** 93

Chapter 1
ISRAEL'S ENEMIES WITHIN

Monday morning of the second day of March 2022 was a shocking and dramatic day for me and many others in the holy land of Israel. I was watching a live-stream broadcast of the third election campaign in a row, and the results were quite alarming—actually, extremely alarming!

The world was already confronting COVID-19, a lethal virus from China, but this news was minor compared to the drama of past elections in Israel. The Israeli–Arab party, *Hareshima Hameshootefet* (the Hareshima Party), won fifteen electoral seats in the Knesset. This was an unheard-of result that would change Israeli politics forever and compromise the state of Israel's security. The party, as mentioned earlier, had won so many electoral seats it became the leader of the opposition bloc in the Knesset and the Israeli Parliament. For Israel, a country surrounded by enemies, this new political situation might be very devastating.

Are you aware that the prime minister must inform the opposition leader about any significant military operation by Israel against its enemies? Until lately, there has been no problem doing so, as the opposition leader was someone who represented a Jewish and Zionist ideology. However, the Hareshima Party base is extremely anti-Zionist, opposing most or even all of the Zionist vision. Also, the party defines the Israeli Defense Force (IDF) as a fascist army that performs atrocities against humanity. It even encourages the International Court System to arrest and charge IDF officers visiting Europe for committing crimes against humanity.

To understand the party's anti-Zionist bias, it is enough to look at its official website, as it is shown right there on the front page.

It will be extremely dangerous for the Prime Minister of Israel to share sensitive materials with a party founded on ideologies such as is the destruction of Israel as a Jewish and Zionist state. How could any prime minister share information with such a party? It would be like sharing military operations and national security information with a hostile force. What would guarantee that this party would keep such important information secret? What are the chances that some of the Knesset minority members would collaborate with Israel's enemies? Since it has happened in the past, what might stop it from happening in the future?

There may be several facts in this chapter that will be new to you. Points that you might never have heard of, showing the acts of treason performed by the Israeli Arabs against the nation of Israel. The Hareshima Party is an Israeli-Arab political party formed from two separate parties. It pays little attention to supporting its voters either socially or economically, being more focused on trying to destroy Israel from the inside by using the Israeli parliament and the international community to portray Israel as a racist regime like the apartheid regime in South Africa.

The title of this book is *Israel's Enemies Within*. Unfortunately, there are many enemies of Israel within the country, coming from the Jewish society in the land today. For example, did you know Israel was almost on the brink of civil war during its journey to independence? Luckily, one noble man's decision prevented a war that could have destroyed Israel for good.

To understand exactly what happened on March 2, 2020, we first need to understand the structure of the Israeli parliament, the Knesset, and how elections and voting work in Israel.

Israel is a parliamentary democracy. The winning party, the one that most people voted for, is granted the opportunity to form a majority in the Israeli parliament, called the "Coalition." The Israeli Knesset is comprised of 120 members, and all the Knesset members belong to the party with whose ideologies they most agree. Unlike the United States (US), there are more than just two major political parties in Israel. Throughout the brief history of the modern state of Israel, the people have voted for smaller parties that represent their ideologies. There are numerous Jewish religious groups, as well as conservative, liberal, Jewish-religious, and minority representative parties, such as the Arab population that lives in Israel.

The winning party forms a coalition of most of the Knesset members; 61 or more are needed as representatives. The party must cooperate with the leaders of the minor parties by giving them governing roles and creating budget streams that serve the needs of the people who elected them. Usually, governing comes with specific agendas based on the needs of the voters who have selected a particular party. For example, the ultra-Orthodox parties have two major parties in Israel: *Yahadut Hatorah* and *Shas*. *Shas* received seventeen electoral seats, with mandates combined. One mandate is equal to 37,000 votes; however, calculations made by the Israeli Central Election Committee, which are made for each national election campaign, can vary. The first ultra-Orthodox party mentioned received seven mandates, while the latter received ten.

Though these two religious parties are not in agreement due to their differing ideologies and several other reasons, they do have several common desires. Of these, as regards governing roles, they are most interested in the Ministry of the Interior position. The main reason for pursuing this office is to maintain the ethnicity of Judaism. Another significant office that they like to acquire in their political negotiations is the Office of the Religions Ministry. Why is it so important to them to be the minister in this office? Simply put, it is because this minister controls the budget sent to different religious institutions in Israel. These elected representatives are aware of the needs of specific institutions, for example, synagogues, religious schools, and religious activities.

The winning party leader must be aware of the needs of each specific party to avoid mistakes when building a coalition. It is a very complicated, sensitive, and creative task, in which each party leader has their own "shadow advisor," who is a person the leader trusts due to their loyalty and ability to communicate with the other parties. The shadow advisor delivers messages, negotiates, and eventually, signs an agreement—a coalition agreement. Amid the jungle of Israeli politics, this is only one example of many such responsibilities. There are so many experiences and stories that come out of every attempt to form a coalition. Most times, however, these agreements do not last the four years until the next election campaign.

The reasons a coalition may fall into a crisis are many—they often involve issues such as economy or ideology, or are even due to personal matters. An excellent example of this is the fact that some parties have promised their voters that they will not form a coalition with Prime Minister Netanyahu. They claim that Netanyahu is involved in corruption (even though he is not guilty) and are taking action against him for personal reasons, including jealousy. After realizing that they will not be able to match Netanyahu's achievements, they have caused a stir among the members of the *Likud* Party, causing them to choose a different party leader. Unfortunately for them, their plan failed and Netanyahu again leads the party and has won the third campaign, just as he has the previous two. Now, Netanyahu is fighting for his good name in court.

With a slightly better understanding of the structure of the Israeli voting and election campaigns, let us now focus on the first enemy: the elections and the voting system itself.

Why is the election system in Israel considered enemy number one? As mentioned at the beginning of this chapter, there are several important reasons behind the rise of the party whose ideology is opposing Israel's sovereignty. This kind of reality is an actual threat to Israel's existence.

This election method benefits minorities in Israel, who use their power to dictate for most of the public. For example, most of the Jews living in the land live quite a secular lifestyle—a sad fact for Jews living in Israel, but it is true. However, the ultra-Orthodox Jewish parties, using their governing power, will not allow public transportation on Saturday. This example indicates how minorities can control the majority's way of life, in that although most people in Israel believe in the day of rest, they would like the option of public transportation on the Sabbath, so that they can have access to the national parks, public sports centers, and designated swimming beaches. However, the religious parties (who represent a minority of people in Israel) are doing all in their power not to allow even select weekend transportation lines to serve the public. So far, no matter how many demands, protests, and lawsuits have been brought to reverse this issue, there is still no designated public transportation in Israel. This struggle involves both national and municipal transportation.

Several more examples can be offered to prove how much influence the minority elected parties have over most of the Israeli population. They influence relationships, entertainment, and the food industry. In Israel, restaurants and food providers must pay a religious kosher supervisor to serve even completely secular customers. At many entertainment events, such as weddings or even religious concerts, the crowd must separate, with the men in one group and women in the another. There are also some public transportation lines that religious travelers dominate. Several cases have shown them forcing women to sit in the back of the bus while the men sit in the front. These parties encourage this phenomenon.

Some secular bus users have fought back against this last case, and won. Several female passengers refused to sit in the back of the buses, even though they were threatened. Through their actions, public pressure brought the Israeli court to rule and forbid this kind of separation on public transportation. Having control over the Ministry of the Interior is essential to the ultra-Orthodox parties for several reasons; for example, it allows them to control who may get married. If an Israeli man wishes to marry a woman whose father is Jewish but whose mother is not, the Ministry of the

Interior will not permit them to marry in a traditionally Orthodox way and will not recognize the offspring of this marriage as Jews. This has caused many children to be considered outcasts in Israeli society, causing them much emotional pain and agony when they become adults and decide to marry and raise families of their own.

Many times, the Minister of the Interior has used their authority to persecute other religious groups and individuals, predominantly Christian and Messianic communities. Unfortunately, from their religious perspective, these communities are their spiritual enemies. For example, they take this view even though one of the Israel's best friends is the Evangelical Church, which has stood with Israel even in challenging times, supporting the land through prayer and coordinating pro-Israel events and donations. Christian and Messianic groups and individuals are persecuted by the Ministry of the Interior, which introduces difficulties into their lives through methods such as deportation, the nullification of work visas, and bullying.

The third reason why the voting system in Israel is enemy number one is that voting for a specific party may bring unknown representatives to the public before they are elected. I know Israel has a high regard for its military and commanding generals, most of whom have jumped on the Israeli political cart. Invariability, these generals are very popular with voters.

Political figures like Benny Gantz, Ehud Barak, Shaul Mofaz, Yitzchak Rabin, and Moshe Dayan came out of the IDF after serving many years as highly ranked officers and enrolled as politicians. As an IDF soldier, Moshe "Bogie" Yaalon, my division commander, swiftly became the Minister of Security after serving the IDF for many years and becoming the highest-ranked officer, the IDF Chief of Staff.

Here's a great story to share with you, one that is known to most Israeli citizens and is based on the facts mentioned earlier. In 1983, a previous high-ranking IDF Chief of Staff, Rafael Eitan (known for his nickname "Raful"), formed his party and launched a campaign based on quite radical right-wing views. Raful was highly favored by most of the people in Israel, as he was a charismatic, magnetic character. He was not just a commander; he was a farmer who loved cultivating his land with his own hands—a simple man, a man of action, and a straight talker. Many people, including myself, adored him. The name of the party he formed was called *Tzomet* (Cross Road). Most of the predictions were that he would get two to three of the mandates needed for the Knesset; however, his party won big, gaining eight mandates. Raful, surprised that he had won so much more decisively than expected, chose the people he found fit for the seats given to him. Those chosen were utterly unknown to the voters. The media called them "The Seven Dwarfs."

Sometimes politics might be funny and exciting, and so it is with this story. One of those unknown politicians was a man named Gonen Segev, who was the energy minister from 1995 to 1996. In 2019, he was caught spying for the fiercest enemy of Israel today: the Islamic Republic of Iran. He was giving them highly sensitive intel and was the one who initiated contact with Iranian intelligence and delivered documents to them that he had received while working as an official. When he was interrogated about why he turned over sensitive information when contacting an intelligence agent, he said that it was all for monetary reasons.

The voters expected Raful to bring their dreams and vision of the land into reality—imagine how disappointed they were with such a shameful outcome. The charismatic Raful is no longer with us, as he was killed in an accident at work. Indeed, I suspect he is rolling in his grave, knowing that he elected such a selfish traitor to his party. Segev is currently serving a life sentence in a high-security prison designated for traitors such as him.

There have been many such situations where voters received results they never envisioned. Therefore, there needs to be another way for the people to vote with much more clarity; the people of Israel deserve it. Especially considering the third reason, as voters should be able to pick their own representatives, not unknown persons.

Another issue concerns time and money. Any election campaign will result in forming a coalition. Forming a multiple coalition partnership is highly difficult and requires creativity and time. Most times, the 21 days granted by the President of Israel to the winning party leader are not enough. In such cases, an extension is granted, or the president gives time and the opportunity for the second party to form a coalition. Some instances in the past have taken less than 21 days; however, in most cases, it takes a few months to create a parliament majority. In the lost elections, we have witnessed the perfect storm: three campaigns without a coalition being formed. So far, therefore, the people have waited for almost two years for a government. In the meantime, they are being governed by a "frozen government" that cannot make crucial decisions relating to any aspect of Israeli society.

This situation causes agony, frustration, and money loss. With each election campaign costing around 2 billion shekels (the Israeli currency) and paid for by the taxpayers, Israel has spent approximately 6 billion shekels on the last three campaigns alone. For a small economy like Israel, this amount is just overwhelming.

The reasons listed above are the primary reasons why Israel's election is causing harm to its people. Therefore, it has to be changed, and the change *has* to come from the people, not from the politicians. Like the US, Israel has a significant political swamp. Swamp creatures are a suitable analogy for the current chaos, as they take advantage of and couldn't care less about people. Therefore, a forceful and uncompromising demand has to come from the streets of Israel until the Knesset hears the message loud and clear.

Previous politicians have attempted to make some minor changes to the voting procedure. However, if the current election process that allows people to be elected anonymously is not taken seriously and stopped, Israel's problems will worsen. Sadly, many elected politicians have grown used to the current reality, and so the swamp continues to exist.

The Israeli people must rise and make change happen. If not, we will experience more and more deterioration, frustration, and even clashes that may lead to violence in Israeli society.

The election method has to be changed. During Israel's brief history, several alternatives were introduced to the Israeli parliament, one of which is the regional voting method. In a nutshell, each region elects its own parliamentary representatives. This election method guarantees that people from all parts of Israel can choose their Knesset representatives. However, this kind of decision has to come from the people: they need to pursue this change. Doing nothing guarantees that nothing will change in a positive way.

Israel has many more enemies to discuss. The next chapter will focus on the Israeli–Arab problem. "Are you persecuting minorities?" you might say. Not at all. Have you heard the story of the ancient city of Troy? Israel is experiencing, on many levels, a Trojan horse coming from this community.

Chapter 2

TROJAN HORSES IN THE ISRAELI KNESSET

(KM Miri Regev: Minister of Culture and Sport of Israel)

As an Israeli man, serving in the Israel Defense Force (IDF) has been one of the highlights of my entire life and is something that I'm incredibly proud of. Looking back, the events I experienced throughout my military service seemed endless. Were there any hardships or challenging times? Absolutely! But I would not substitute my military experience for anything. During my service, I learned so much about self-discipline, hard work, and serving others. By operating in the IDF, I realized our military is one of the best in the world due to its history, achievements, and perhaps most importantly, its respect for humanity and human life.

A harrowing number of combat soldiers who took part in Israel's wars and military operations lost their lives. They did their best not to shoot innocent civilians, even when the enemy would use them as human shields. As mentioned above, the list of my experiences is long and very painful. However, I can share one that reflects the quality of this beautiful army. In 1989, while Israel was dealing with riots, with protestors throwing stones at Israeli vehicles and even using Molotov cocktails to injure Israeli civilians and soldiers, our units worked around the clock to maintain order. During one of our missions, we were ordered to enter a village in the middle of the night and arrest several of its residents who were suspected of violent activities.

One of the troop's commanders entered a building to arrest the prime suspects. Unfortunately, the suspect himself heard the noise; he sneaked behind the officer and pulled the trigger of the officer's weapon. The shots fired woke the entire village, whereupon the villagers threw stones and Molotov cocktails at us, which they had prepared before our arrival. In the meantime, our officer was fighting for his life. The terrorist tried grabbing the officer's AR-15, attempting to stab him while doing so. This was a one-on-one battle.

Eventually, the officer overcame the terrorist and knocked him out. Both of them were injured. What happened next will remain in my memory for the rest of my life. I was one of the first to enter that building and noticed both men being taken care of at the same time by our troop's paramedics. The terrorist was being treated fairly by the military paramedics. He was experiencing difficulty breathing, and I saw the effort the paramedics put into ensuring he could breathe correctly and independently. Being an eyewitness to this event made me realize just how humane the IDF is.

Why share this story with you? Namely, because it demonstrates, through a single incident, just how much respect the IDF has for human lives and how much dignity it offers them. And not just in Israel—were a natural disaster, such as an earthquake or volcanic eruption, to happen anywhere in the world, the IDF would be one of the first to send trauma and rescue units to help. It even offers help to enemy countries. For example, in 2003, 26,000 Iranian people were killed in a 6.6 magnitude earthquake in Bam, Iran. The Israelis offered to help the Iranians by sending the IDF's special rescue units, but their offer was rejected. These same rescue units eventually traveled to other disaster areas, such as Haiti and Turkey, bringing relief, encouragement, and help. Sadly, several Israeli Knesset parties have dared to label the IDF as a fascist military. They have also called the IDF officers and soldiers "child killers," among many other unjustified comments. These parties are those that represent the Arab community in Israel. Some of the Knesset members (KM) genuinely represent the needs of their voters; however, some use the political stage to fight Israel from within, from the Knesset pulpit.

Azmi Bishara, a member of the Knesset in 1999, was born in Nazareth in 1956 to a Christian–Arab Catholic family. His actions against Israel did not make him a saint; indeed, to this day, he cannot walk on the waters of the Sea of Galilee just because he was born in Nazareth. As a Knesset member, he was the founder of the Balad Party. His father worked as an official in the Ministry of Health in Israel.

In 1975, Bishara studied for a psychology degree at the University of Haifa. He also studied law at the Hebrew University of Jerusalem. He became an advocate for socialism, believing that communism would resolve the issues in Israeli–Arab society. He went on to study philosophy at Humboldt University in East Berlin, with the city still divided following the aftermath of the second World War. In 1986, Bishara came back to the land of his birth and studied at Birzeit University, near the city of Ramallah. He founded the Balad Party, whose full name (*Brit Leumit Democratit*) means National Democratic Unity. At its core, the party wishes to eliminate Israel's Jewish identity, renounce its Zionist ideology, and destroy its nuclear power.

Bishara was elected in the campaign for the Knesset in 1996, receiving two mandates. In 2001, he visited Syria, considered to be an enemy of Israel, to take part in a memorial service for the deceased Syrian President, Hafez Al Assad. Hassan Nasrallah, a Hezbollah terrorist from Beirut, Lebanon, attended the ceremony, followed by an Iranian delegation. During the memorial service, Bishara delivered a hateful speech against Israel. His KM immunity prevented him from being arrested at the airport when he returned home. However, he was indicted, and his immunity was removed following that act of treason. Even so, he was still permitted to run a campaign for the next elections, made possible only because the Israeli Supreme Court reversed the decision of the Israeli Elections Committee, which had barred him from campaigning.

Though Bishara was forbidden from visiting countries that did not have diplomatic relationships with Israel, especially Lebanon and Syria, he went to Damascus again, taking several more KMs with him. During his visit, he declared his support for Syria, encouraged terrorist organizations such as Hamas and Hezbollah, and spoke about continuing armed fighting with Israel. Following this development, the Attorney General of Israel permitted a criminal investigation to be launched against Bishara. On March 23, 2007, Bishara crossed the border from Israel into Jordan, and never returned to Israel.

On April 22, 2007, Bishara resigned from the Israeli parliament through the Israeli consul in Cairo, Egypt. However, since his resignation, he has continued to collaborate against Israel.

In the summer of 2006, during the Lebanon war, Israel discovered that Bishara, while acting as a KM, contacted a Hezbollah agent, giving him information about strategic facilities in Israel to launch rockets and missiles. Further investigation revealed that Bishara informed the leader of Hezbollah how to use counteractions to prevent an assassination. Bishara received $500,000 for that effort, which came directly from Hezbollah and other terrorist organizations. He then used the help of several Arab money changers from East Jerusalem to launder that money.

Following these actions and other crimes, Bishara wandered between the capital cities of the Arab world, using his academic knowledge to lecture in universities and talk about the Israeli–Arab conflict from his perspective. Bishara was invited to participate as a commentator for the Arab cable television company Al Jazeera, and was a writer for the well-known Arab newspaper Al Ahram. He was also hired as an advisor for the Emir of Qatar.

In June 2000, Israel withdrew from the safety zone that the Israelis had created in Lebanon. Bishara commented:

> Hezbollah has won! And, for the first time since 1967 (The Six-Day War), we have tasted victory. It is the right of all Hezbollah to be proud of these achievements and to humiliate Israel. The latter has been defeated and was forced to leave South Lebanon; this is the truth! Lebanon, the weakest of all the other Arab nations, has launched a small model of military operations for us to look deeply into and to conclude essential conclusions that will lead to success and victory!

Later, after returning from one of his treacherous visits to Syria, he said to an Israeli journalist, "Syria is an enemy of the State of Israel, not mine! I cannot and will not call Syria my enemy! Even if you crucify me, I will not say it, ever!"

Do you think that KM Bishara's acts of treason are a rare case among the honored Arab Knesset members? Before continuing, I want to emphasize that honest Arab KM representatives genuinely do their best to promote the needs of the Israeli–Arab communities. Most of them are honored citizens of Israel, and I have met some wonderful Arabs from Israel who are my friends. Some of them are even my brothers and sisters, with faith in Yeshua, the Messiah of Israel. My friends and I are totally in agreement that we need to uproot those who want to cause chaos in our society, whether they are Arabs or Jews.

With these concepts in mind, allow me to introduce Hannin Zoabi to you. She is another KM whose notorious acts will upset you and leave you shaking your head with disbelief.

Zoabi was born in Nazareth, Israel, on May 23, 1969. She was a member of the Balad Party, which was eventually co-joined by the Hareshima Party. She was born to a Sunni Muslim family that was involved in Israel's struggle for independence. Her relative, Seif A-din Zoabi, was a member of the *Hagana*, an armed Jewish force established to protect Jewish settlements from the Arab gang members who attacked the settlements. Through his actions—that is, by joining forces and protecting the land from these gangs—he saved his family. However, Hannin did not follow the example of her heroic relative, instead choosing a different path.

Zoabi joined the Balad party in 1997. She was considered to be Bishara favorite disciple, visiting him in Jordan several times after he escaped to Israel. She was elected as the party's representative in Nazareth and became a KM in the 2009 elections. This was the first time that an Arab woman from an Arab party had become a KM. After her election, Zoabi did not wait long to unleash her anti-Israeli ideology with the help of hostile international organizations, including the well-known Boycott, Divestment, and Sanctions (BDS) organization. This organization declared an economic boycott on Israeli produce to destroy Israel's economy.

In May 2010, a Turkish Pro-Palestinian Radical Islamic organization named IHH organized a cruise from Turkey to the Gaza strip. The IHH, an Islamic terrorist organization according to Israel and the Netherlands, claimed that the purpose of the cruise was to bring humanitarian aid to Gaza. Since the Gaza Strip, controlled by the terrorist organization Hamas, was not experiencing a humanitarian crisis, this was a false claim. Back then, there was tension between Israel and Hamas. Hamas had launched missiles and sent terrorist units to cause harm to the Israeli settlements across the border. However, Israel always supplied basic necessities to prevent any humanitarian crisis on the strip. The IHH's primary goal was to break the naval siege on Gaza; the purpose of the security siege was to control terrorist actions from the sea and to embarrass Israel internationally.

Zoabi flew to Turkey to join this cruise for provocation purposes only. The name of the ship was "Marmara." The Israelis were aware that, ideologically, the IHH was a terrorist Islamic organization. However, they also knew that there were civilians from several European countries on board. Therefore, the security forces stopped the ship, using non-lethal weapons, once it had entered Israel's territorial waters.

The Israeli Navy communicated using the ship's radio channels, demanding that the ship leave Israeli territorial waters. A comment by one of the crew members navigating the vessel was recorded as being "Go back to Auschwitz," while the ship continued toward Gaza. The Israeli Navy had no choice but to take control of the ship. Armed with non-lethal weapons such as rubber bullets, special unit soldiers were brought down by helicopter cables to the ship's upper deck. What happened next was complete chaos. Soldiers were beaten with batons and sticks, and some were stabbed. One was thrown from an upper deck to a lower deck. The violent mob captured an Israeli soldier. When one traveler used a firearm, the Israelis had no choice but to use lethal weapons to take control of the ship and rescue the injured soldiers, who were still being beaten even after being injured. Once the Israeli forces took control of the boat, the captive soldier was released.

The results were severe: nine Turkish citizens were killed and ten Israeli soldiers were injured, two of them severely.

Zoabi called the operation a "massacre" and denied seeing any weapons on the boat, even though some pictures were taken on board before the Israeli forces arrived that showed her with some activists holding sticks and knives. The Marmara was brought to the shores of Israel. After searching the ship, many blades, metal rods, and other weapons were found. The Israelis also discovered gas masks, bulletproof vests (with Turkish police emblems on them), and several improvised firearms. This horrific event reached the international news and commentators, who accused Israel of the supposed massacre. Recep Tayyip Erdogan, the President of Turkey, called the event "a crime against humanity," discontinued diplomatic connections with Israel for three years, and encouraged the Turkish people to boycott Israeli products.

Another aftereffect of this event involves the US. The then-United States President Barack Hussein Obama came to Israel for an official visit three years after the Marmara event. As he was boarding Air Force One to leave, he asked Netanyahu to call Turkey's president and apologize for the entire event. Netanyahu did so, and the President of Turkey accepted the apology and restored relations with Israel after the Israelis promised to pay compensation to the victims' families.

To my knowledge, looking at the connections between Israel and the USA, there has never been a case where a US president has put political pressure on an Israeli prime minister to apologize to another nation, or to a nation's leader, for any crisis. That unpresidential behavior by Obama revealed several facts about him as a person. The first was his personal hostility toward Netanyahu. He used his position as the President of the US to politically pressure and humiliate Netanyahu, demonstrating the personal conflict between the two men. Second, while most US administration guidelines advise the use of intermediaries when taking sides, this case provides evidence for the theory that Obama has a deep Islamic faith and supports the needs of Islamic countries.

Let us now go back to Zoabi, as there is much more to share about the aftermath of the attack. KM Zoabi said to the media that she saw no weapons on board while cruising, and showed no remorse nor regret for calling the event a massacre. Her outrageous actions and comments before, during, and after this dramatic event led the Israeli Minister of the Interior, Eli Yishai, to revoke Zoabi's Israeli citizenship, which action the Israeli General Attorney blocked.

Zoabi has denied what was clear to all. However, after analyzing the vast number of weapons and the pictures and videos of activists presenting their guns and saying anti-Israeli slogans, it is utterly clear that Zoabi was aware of it.

On July 13, 2010, the Knesset chairperson removed Zoabi from the Knesset chamber due to her provocative behavior. While she was being escorted out, she struck an usher. Her international anti-Israeli efforts did not end with the Marmara events. Zoabi wrote an introduction for the book *Palestinians in Israel* by the British author Ben White, stating that "Zionism is a racial, colonial plan." She has also expressed her objections to a moment of silence for the memory of the eleven Israeli athletes kidnapped and murdered during the Olympic Games in Munich, and has compared Israel to a terrorist regime. After the terrorist attack on Israeli tourists in Burgas, Bulgaria, Zoabi said, "Israel is not the victim, even when its civilians are getting murdered. Israel is always to be blamed because of its occupation. If there were no occupation, none of that would have happened."

In June 2014, Israel was challenged with one of the most dramatic and sad events in its history. Three Israeli teenagers were kidnapped and killed by terrorists, who used pistols equipped with silencers. The entire event was audio recorded. One of the kidnapped young men phoned Moked 100 (the Israeli 911), and said that he had been abducted. These were his last words. The audio recorded several shots from a silenced firearm. Listening to the audio is horrific. Not knowing that Moked 100 was still listening to the distress call, the kidnappers increased the vehicle's radio volume while shooting the teenagers and singing joyful Arab songs following their murderous act. Zoabi, during an interview on the radio, claimed that the murderers were not terrorists. She added, "though I disagree with them, I can see why they have done it following the fact that they couldn't change their oppressed reality ... They are doing this so that Israel would come to its senses a little."

On October 8, 2015, Zoabi was interviewed by a website that identified with the terrorist organization Hamas. In the interview, she encouraged a violent uprising against Israel, saying

Hundreds of thousands of worshipers need to go to the Al-Aqsa Mosque to stop an Israeli conspiracy that will destroy the lives of many in Jerusalem. Today, only a few are resisting, but national support is needed. Thousands of our people coming will bring a real uprising and victory!

Following these comments and many more, Netanyahu demanded that the General Attorney of Israel, Yehuda Weinstein, open a criminal investigation against Zoabi for her incitement of violence.

In January 2019, Zoabi announced she was ending her political career and would no longer run campaigns for the Knesset. According to news reports, there are several investigations against her: for forgery, using a forged document, and laundering money. Although Zoabi is a very anti-Israeli figure, one of her family members is an excellent Zionist. Muhammad Zoabi speaks out against his provocative relative frequently. For that solidarity with the state of Israel, he has received several threats in his life. During the history of Israel, there were several Israeli Arabs that supported the Jewish right to claim the land that was taken away from them a long time ago. Sometimes, they even helped Jewish underground organizations fight the British while they occupied the land. For example, the village Abu-Ghosh, located between Israel and Jerusalem during the British rule of Israel, refused to join the Arab gangs to fight the Jews. The village settlers even hid Jewish underground warriors from the British.

Former KM Zoabi has polluted the minds of many with her actions and further damaged the relationship between the Arab and Israeli communities, who are trying to live as equal citizens and peacefully and tranquilly together, with their utmost desires being to pursue happiness and prosperity. Several more members of her party have been provocative during Knesset committees, political disputes, and even in war and conflict between Israel and its enemies. For example, while Israel was fighting Hamas to prevent missiles trained on the Israeli cities and settlements from launching, KM Jamal Zahalka called Netanyahu "the angel of death," "a war criminal," and "a baby killer." On July 14, 2004, during a brief meeting with *** Danino, the Israeli Chief of Police, Zahalka called Danino a "murderer," and stated that "his hands are stained with blood." For these comments, he was removed from the briefing chamber. His anti-Israeli comments, along with the statements and actions of his party members, are many.

Following these actions and comments, the fundamental question is "Does the KM's behavior contribute to the Israeli–Arab acts of terrorism against Israel?"

The events described in the following paragraphs will speak for themselves.

On September 9, 2001, Muhammed Shucker Chabishi, from the village Abu-Snan, detonated himself at the train station in Nahariya (a city in the north of Israel). As a result, three were killed and 92 were injured. Chabishi's son was arrested on suspicion of collaborating with his father. Two weeks before the suicide attack, the son ran away and hid from Israeli security, so as not to get caught before the attack planned by his father.

Ahmed Jaabar, an Israeli Arab married to a Jewish woman, collaborated with a suicide bomber and drove him to a mall in Netanya, Israel. On May 18, 2001, Jaabar used his Israeli-licenced vehicle to smuggle the terrorist from Tul-Karem, in the Palestinian Authority, crossing the IDF checkpoints to the Israeli mall. As a result, the suicide bomber entered an Israeli mall, detonating the bomb he was carrying. The sad outcome of this was that five people were killed and 100 were injured, some severely. Jaabar smuggled the terrorist for only 100 Shekels ($25), confessing that the person he took with him looked pretty suspicious since he was wearing a thick coat during a scorching day in the summer. Jaabar did nothing to stop the attack from happening.

On June 1, 2001, a suicide terrorist detonated himself in a dance club called "the Dolphinarium." Twenty-one young people were killed and 106 were injured. The terrorist was driven by a cab driver from Jaffa, a city located very near to Tel Aviv, in which Israeli Jews and Arabs had lived together for decades. The Israeli cab driver, Nadi Mahmud, was aware that he was helping a terrorist. He drove to a nearby mosque and helped the terrorist hide. He had also helped to prepare the terrorist's resting place before the attack. He was found guilty, but was sentenced to only twelve years in prison.

Buheiza Saadi, a 25-year-old man from Sakhnin, Israel, was sentenced to 16 months in prison because he knew about a planned attack in Jerusalem and failed to report it.

The Israeli General Security Service (GSS) has reported that there were 104 organized terrorist plans between 2001 and 2004 performed by 200 Israeli Arabs, which killed 136 Israelis.

During the rise of the bloodthirsty terrorist organization ISIS, there was an increase in support for ISIS among the Arab population in Israel. The young supported this terrible organization, but so did individuals of all ages and genders in Muslim Arab Society. A rising and alarming number of Israeli civilians joined the ISIS ranks during the battles in Syria and Iraq. The journey to join the group was quite a peaceful one, and flights from Israel to Turkey were incredibly economical. After landing in Turkey, where there is hardly any border control, it was easy for these volunteers to get to Syria and join ISIS. During the battles, the men learned how to operate assault rifles, artillery and tanks, and even to build bombs.

Israeli intelligence could not afford to take any actions against that ticking time bomb. There was no way that Israel would allow ISIS cells to form among Israeli citizens, as the outcome would have been horrifying.

In 2014, twelve citizens who left to join ISIS and fought in Syria and Iraq were arrested. They did not come from any specific location; they were reported as coming from the north side of Israel, the Negev, and the East

Jerusalem area. In 2015, forty-four were arrested, and in 2016, seventy were arrested. All were Israeli citizens.

During an investigation, most of those arrested confessed that they were taught methods of spreading radical Islamic ideology while in Syria. For example, they were trained to use martial arts and knives for killing purposes and learned how to build bombs and deal with different explosives.

The idea of joining ISIS was so popular among the population that one person from a town called Jaljulia used a paraglider to cross the border on the Golan Heights, Israel, to Syria. An Israeli intern doctor named Athman Abu-Alkian, who used to work at Barzilai, a hospital in Ashkelon City, joined ISIS and was killed in Syria. The whole family, including his children, left the town of Sakhnin among ISIS. A Jewish convert to Islam, Vladimir Mazlevski, revealed his intentions to join ISIS, but was stopped while attempting to leave Israel and get to Syria via Turkey.

Although Israel is trying to cover this, these minorities among the Arab communities are an actual threat to Israel's security. Israel is doing its best to protect its citizens from other citizens of its own. Sounds conflicting? It is! But the facts speak for themselves.

The Israelis witnessed one of the most horrific and most communicated terrorist attacks in the new year of 2016. Nasha'at Malcham, a 31-year-old man from the town of Ar'ara in the Galilee, traveled to Tel Aviv with a vintage Italian machine gun, a Spectre M4, hidden in his backpack. Security cameras in various shops show Malcham walking into a grocery store, and while exiting the store, start to shoot the people around him. Two people were killed, while seven were injured. The security cameras show Malcham walking in a very unsuspicious manner before the shooting. The GSS recognized this pattern of behavior as a person who has been well trained by a terrorist organization for this task.

Immediately after the shooting, which occurred in Dizengoff Street, Malcham ran away from the scene. He stopped a taxicab and asked the driver to drive north. When the driver realized he had a terrorist on board, he refused to take him to his desired location. For that, the cab driver, who was also an Israeli Arab, paid with his life. Malcham took the wheel after killing the cab driver. He headed north, and left the vehicle behind with his mobile phone, using other ways to escape. At first, the Israeli security forces thought Malcham was hiding in the city of Tel Aviv, as they presumed that there might be another terrorist attack at a tourist location in the city, which meant that many citizens of Tel Aviv did not leave home for several days after the attack.

However, intel determined that Malcham went north, since he made the big mistake of stealing the cab driver's smartwatch. That fact helped the Israeli intelligence put surveillance on his approximate location by monitoring the stolen watch.

After a tense week, the terrorist was found in his hometown, in the house belonging to his parents. Security forces surrounded the perimeter and told him to come out and surrender. However, the terrorist responded by firing on them. The Israeli special forces immediately neutralized him, and none of the security personnel were hurt.

In the aftermath, an investigation revealed that Malcham had stolen and used his father's weapon, which he had reported as lost right after the terrorist attack. The investigation also revealed that collaborators had helped the terrorist, taking him to a hiding place and supplying him with a TV, a cell phone, food, candy, and coffee throughout the week he was in hiding. All the collaborators caught were Israeli Arabs. This terrorist event brought about a thorough discussion among the security forces in Israel and the Israeli public. Many topics and questions were raised on the radio and via other broadcasts, such as:

1. Is the holding of illegal weapons by the population sufficiently policed?
2. What restrictions are put in place when the Israeli intelligence determines the presence of radicalization among Israeli citizens, especially young Muslims?
3. Is the Arab community in Israel doing enough to stop the "bad weeds" in its society?

Other suggestions have included removing restrictions from handgun carry licensing and providing much quicker permit and handgun purchasing discounts, especially to soldiers with combat backgrounds serving the IDF and with moral standards. Some people have suggested increasing the penalty for collaborators, even as far as a death sentence.

In the Arab community, there is a massive number of weapons that have become illegal. Some of those weapons have been possessed by families for generations. In Israel, a weapon is licenced weapon is entitled to the owner alone. Once they pass, the gun is illegal and must be turned in to the authorities. However, in most cases, the weapon is not turned over. The security forces claim that most of the handguns and rifles are used for underworld reasons; that is, to settle matters between criminals relating to drugs, gambling, or prostitution.

In 2018, in Arab society alone, the number of shooting victims climbed to its peak, with over 70 people killed by guns. Ballistics and other criminal investigations prove the shots came from either illegal vintage firearms or from weapons stolen from the IDF.

Even the Arab parties in the Knesset were begging the police to enforce the laws and use the police force to search for illegal weapons. The police undertook some operations, before realizing that they found only the tip of the iceberg. The number of illegal guns found is staggering and frightening. According to the previous Minister of National Security, Gilead Ardan, 90% of the illicit weapons were the result of smuggling or had been been stolen from the IDF. Ardan listed several underground illegal weapons factories, some of which were connected to smuggling activities emanating from Lebanon, Jordan, and Egypt.

The Palestinian Authority has also contributed to this industry by providing improvised weapons, including refurbished guns and grenades. Ardan even mentioned price lists. For example, a Carl Gustav m/45 submachine gun's market value is 6,500 shekels, while the price of a grenade in the market is 1,500 shekels. A handgun sells for 10,000 shekels, while a C4 explosive brick is 7,000 shekels. The criminals first choice of gun is an IDF assault rifle; the price of a stolen gun in this underworld market is around 7,000 shekels.

Despite all the research conducted on the specific subject of illegal weapon possession, none of those who deal with Israeli security have dared to give a particular number. However, as the British say, "the proof is in the pudding." The numbers are too staggering!

The number of female victims in Israeli society is rising. Conservative family codes and the fact that many women are becoming more Westernized has resulted in many murder cases, committed using lethal weapons. The number of women murdered by their family members and others for this reason is eighteen times higher than the number of Israeli Jewish women murdered as a result of domestic violence. As mentioned above, Israel is aware of the signs, but the current preventative actions are not enough.

Although Israel's political and judicial objections aimed at resolving the issue of illegal weapons within Arab society are correct, most of the time, the country simply ignores them.

There has to be an awakening of the people in the land—Jews, Arabs, and other minorities—and they need to rise and demand solutions. The current and future governments of Israel need to understand, from the public folders, that this issue is crucial and needs to be resolved; if it is not, it will soon bite Israel in the back. Unfortunately, the existing rising political power within the Arab parties cares more about embarrassing Israel politically or internationally than it does about taking care of this fundamental problem in Arab society. Therefore, something has to be done: the change has to come from the people themselves. If not, there might be a real danger to Israel's safety and its survival.

The rest of this chapter will discuss a pre-modern Israeli historical figure who most Israeli-Arabs adore as an Islamic religious leader. Hajj Amin Al-Husseini, the Mufti of Jerusalem, is a highly revered and adored figure who many believe should be followed as an example.

Al-Husseini was born in 1895. In 1921, he became the Mufti (an Islamic legal expert empowered to give rulings in religious matters) of Jerusalem through the use of leverage and various threats against the British military rulers in the city. He held this position until 1937. He was the superior leader of the Israeli Arabs during the British mandate. No other religious figure has matched his influence over the Israeli Arabs; this includes his stance that the right of a Jewish state to exist should be nullified. Al-Husseini was known for his anti-Semitism, his resistance to Zionism, and his encouragement of attacks on Jewish settlements in Israel and other Arab countries.

This religious figure was so hostile to the Jewish people and to Zionism that, immediately after assuming his role as a mufti, he wrote an Islamic fatwa (decree) forbidding Jews from coming to pray at the Western Wall and banning them from bringing certain items with them (Torah scrolls, prayer books, and other Jewish religious objects). He also organized conferences on topics such as "Destroying the plan of the Jews to destroy Al-Aqsa Mosque, and building the Jewish temple."

On November 1, 1928, Al-Husseini officiated the above-named conference, which was attended by 700 representatives coming from all over the land. In this conference, he revealed his support for removing, by force, any Jews who came to settle in the Holy Land. His speeches were sent to the Arab countries and even to London. Unfortunately, this conference gathering led to several massacres throughout the land; 133 Jews were murdered as a result, and 339 wounded. The mob also destroyed several Jewish settlements. The Jewish community in Hebron, which had existed for hundreds of years, was eliminated. Sixty-seven Jews were murdered, children were slaughtered right in front of their parents, some were burned alive, women and girls were raped, and Jewish homes were looted. All of this occurred while the British watched and did nothing to help; they interfered only when the mob attacked them. A British soldier fired one shot into the air, and they scattered.

Al-Husseini reached the apex of his hatred toward the Jewish people and the pioneering settlers by meeting with Adolf Hitler in Berlin, Germany. This meeting was in May 1930, when the mufti contacted the German foreign ministry, protesting British policy and claiming that Britain was protecting the Zionists. In 1933, Al-Husseini officially visited the German consular in Jerusalem, because the Nazi party had come into power in Germany. During that visit, he expressed his wish for the spread of Nazism all over the world. The German consul understood Al-Husseini wanted to collaborate with the Nazi killing machine in exterminating Jews, since he gave several suggestions relating to dealing with Zionists and the Jewish people. Therefore, he arranged for the historic meeting with Adolf Hitler. In 1935, Al-Husseini received funds from fascists in Italy to poison the waters of Tel Aviv. The mission, which the British intelligence prevented, was to purchase several cyanide tanks and help German paratroopers land in Jericho and guide them to the water source. Eventually, the British captured the platoon, and the only damage caused was to some pipes, which the British fixed. There were no casualties.

This Jewish-hating person did not stop there in his collaboration with the Nazi regime. After he met with Hitler in November 1941, Al-Husseini represented the Nazis in Israel. He formed the Boy Scouts, similar to the Hitler Youth, complete with Nazi uniforms, flags, and symbols. During his meeting with Hitler in Berlin, he offered his support to help exterminate the Jews in Arab countries. He suggested his influence over the Arab world as a tool of Nazi propaganda, promoting fascism and inciting the mobs to harm Jewish people. Husseini took advantage of the fact that most of the Arab regimes were unstable. Using AM radio broadcasts, he unleashed his Islamic-fascist propaganda. He broadcast for four years, with 80 Nazi assistants assigned to help him with his broadcasting. From a small town near Berlin, he published propaganda in the Arabic language, encouraging riots with the aim of promoting Nazism and murdering Jews. His incitement led to riots in Iraq, Syria, and Jordan, as well as in Israel, which was under the British mandate.

There were several reports of mobs killing Jews while raping their wives and children and looting and burning their homes. Al-Husseini called on the Israeli Arabs to be prepared for the Germans to conquer the land and take its rule from the British and to act accordingly by massacring the Jews.

Al-Husseini also was successful at helping to establish a death squad that would be assigned the task to kill the Jews in the land once it had been conquered by the Nazis. This squad was stationed in Athens, where it waited for the Nazi forces to conquer Egypt before moving from there up to Israel. Fortunately, this plan failed; the land remained safe, and the Jewish community in the country was spared. However, during the war, Al-Husseini contacted the Nazis and asked them to extend their extermination of the Jews in Europe. From his satanic point of view, if the Nazis eliminated all the Jews in Europe, they could not come to Israel to destroy the mosque in Jerusalem and rebuild their temple.

His influence brought sad results, including the massacre of a community of Hungarian Jews, a staggering number of more than a million Jews: men, women, and children. Al-Husseini even jeopardized the plan to exchange 20,000 German soldiers for 5,000 Jews and send the Jews to be exterminated. Furthermore, he enlisted Bosnian Muslim soldiers in the *Schutzstaffel* (SS) ranks.

The SS was considered the personal security force of Hitler's inner circle. Through his actions, Al-Husseini proved how deeply involved he was in Nazi circles during WW2. For that "success," he received a medal of honor from the Nazi criminal, Heinrich Himmler, that ranked him as equivalent to an SS general. The mufti also translated Hitler's book, *Mein Kampf*, into Arabic; to this day, this book is still considered a bestseller throughout the Middle East. Thankfully, after the war, Al-Husseini was unable to return to Israel or most of the Arab countries, since he had collaborated with the Nazis in trying to cause revolutions by inciting the mobs. Eventually, he moved to Lebanon and died there in 1974.

Understanding Al-Husseini is crucial to understanding the current conflict, as to this day, the Arabs have a high regard for his teachings. His activities reveal an incredible darkness; however, neither his followers nor politicians representing Arabs ever mention his incriminating past or his affiliation with Hitler and the Nazis.

Several crucial questions should be asked, therefore, as this figure is still very influential among both religious and social Arabs in Israel. First, why is it that no one discusses this man's past? Of course, Arab politicians have had no problem with accusing Israel of being a fascist, discriminatory country; however, they have never confessed and apologized for their dark pasts, and all are highly revered and never criticized.

Reflecting on the above question, if Al-Husseini is such an adored figure who is considered to be perfect, could it be that, inside the minds of those who follow him, lies the desire to continue exterminating the Jews, clearing them from the land?

The historical fact is that the Nazis were socialist; Hitler used socialist ideas to establish his party. So, could this be why all Arab parties in the Knesset are politically socialist, hiding a Nazi, anti-Semite ideology? Why have Arab historians not told the truth to the Arab world about Al-Husseini's actions during the second World War?

The German people have taken responsibility for the murder of Jews and other people. Why is it that the Arab KM members refuse to take responsibility for the actions of a leader they seem to hold up as a role model? These facts are firmly established in recent history and are easy for anyone to find and recognize. It seems very unwise to hold someone up as a role model for your children if they fully cooperated with Hitler in trying to exterminate the Jewish people.

Many, or even most of the Israeli Arabs, see themselves as Palestinians. Although this book's intention is not to discuss the Israeli–Palestinian conflict, a few matters must be addressed. First, let me be quick to add that I have nothing against the Palestinian people; rather, I am referring to those who have been radicalized by extremist Islamic ideology. Most of the Palestinian people want to live in peace and raise their families. However, they often find themselves at the mercy of malicious bullies such as the Palestine Liberation Organization (PLO) and Hamas. The current Palestinian Authority leader, Mahmoud Abbas, or Kunya Abu Mazen, has a unique academic degree. He is probably the only person in the world that has a doctorate on the topic of Holocaust denial. His doctorate thesis claims the Holocaust did not result in six million Jews dead, while most of the world's researchers know the numbers as fact. There is nothing as anti-Semitic as to deny the Holocaust ever happened. Abbas, in this shameful doctoral work, claims that the Holocaust was fabricated and was a plan of the Zionists and the Nazis, working together to establish a Jewish state. This proclamation is a horrific and despicable claim that shows he is a sick anti-Semite and an evil man.

How can the Israeli Arabs and the Palestinians see this person as a suitable leader to negotiate peace with Israel? Does it not sound absurd that a Holocaust denier could reasonably negotiate peace with the nation whose history he refuses to accurately recognize?

Indeed, you, dear reader, must have your own questions by now.

Al-Husseini was not the only person among the Israeli Arabs who collaborated with the Nazis; other names can be added to this "honorable list," such as Russem Chaldi, Jamal Husseini, and Whatzfi Kamel, each with his own evil expression of hate toward the Jews and against Zionist pioneers in particular.

This chapter will conclude with a quote by Al-Husseini, in which he compares Nazism to Islam. We had better take his words seriously, since he was a

Sunni Islamic scholar and lived among the Nazis for a while, being elevated and promoted in their circles. The quote is: "There is a great similarity between Nazism and Islam. Therefore, for the Arab countries to adopt Nazism is natural."

The list of the in-house enemies of Israel is just at its beginning, and there is more to see in the next chapters. The following chapter will focus on the relationships between Israel and a community in the Jewish world called the ultra-Orthodox community. There is so much to say about this community, and whether they themselves see it, they too are an enemy within the state of Israel. If you want a reason why Israel has had to endure three election campaigns (and maybe even a fourth or fifth campaign), you will find the next chapter quite interesting.

Chapter 3

THANK GOD THE BIBLE WAS NOT WRITTEN BY RELIGIOUS PEOPLE

The Israeli Defense Force (IDF) is the number-one melting pot of my nation. Millions of Israelis, male and female, have served in various branches of the IDF, taking with them life lessons, discipline, and even their life spouses. In addition, tens of thousands of married couples met while serving in the Israeli military. That was not the case for me, but it is good to mention it.

Growing up in Israel, the military is a national army. You can walk down a street in any major city and see a soldier in uniform. As a person who lives in the Diaspora, I see United States (US) soldiers only frequently; however, in Israel, if you go to an outdoor activity without noticing a soldier, something may well be wrong! In most cases, the soldiers carry their fully automatic assault rifles, which is a pretty intimidating sight for European or US tourists, but a common thing to see for Israelis. The soldiers' presence is a reality that all Israelis understand, and no Israeli can imagine Israel without the IDF. Consider this: the Israeli army is the only army in the world where a father, his son, his daughter, and even his grandson may serve simultaneously, all throughout the year, since those who have served in the full-time military are often called on to help the military reserve duty until the age of 50, so it is likely that their children may be on regular duty.

The IDF is the primary source of high-level politicians, especially for the position of prime minister, security officials, and even foreign ministers. Some of the politicians that have come to politics following military careers and positions as high-ranking officers are Moshe Dayan, Yitzchak Rabin, Ariel Sharon, and Shaul Mofaz. Since Israel, sadly, is still living by the sword, politicians with military careers are highly respected, well regarded, and voted into influential positions in Israeli politics. For example, in the last elections, the number-one nominee to campaign against Benjamin Netanyahu was the previous IDF Chief of Staff, Benny Gantz. Gantz was chosen as a nominee by many, and primarily by those who were the enemies of Netanyahu, as Gantz had finished his military service with a much higher rank than Netanyahu.

I must mention that Netanyahu used his military background to promote himself politically, not just through his military records, but also using his deceased brother's memory. Benjamin's brother, Yonatan Netanyahu, known more often by his nickname, Yoni Netanyahu, was the commander of an elite force that rescued hostages from Uganda back in 1976. This counter-terrorist operation occurred because of an Israeli hostage crisis that occurred after Palestinian terrorists hijacked an Air France plane and landed in Entebbe, Uganda. Israel decided not to negotiate with terrorists and sent a single unit to rescue the hostages. This operation was quite a success, recovering most of the hostages, and is one of the most successful counter-terrorism and hostage rescue operations ever conducted, with only a few hostages sadly killed. However, the most tragic event was that Yoni, the commander of the force and an excellent officer, was killed during this operation. His heroism echoes even today, and the people will remember him forever. Benjamin Netanyahu used his brother's memory to promote himself politically. These are just minor examples of how deeply the IDF is ingrained into the reality of Israeli society.

Although, in Israel, serving in the military is a part of the norm, there is an entire community that has been completely opposed to being in the IDF, right from Israel's first day of independence. In any society, there are exceptions to the rule. The IDF has its standards and terms that state who may serve in the military. In most cases, teenagers with criminal records cannot join the IDF unless a specific program within the military is designed for them. The mentally disabled, or those addicted to narcotics like heroin, are also not accepted.

However, in this case, it is an entire community that is wholly opposed to joining and serving in the military. They refuse to carry the burden shouldered by the rest of Israeli society, and they fight against Zionist ideas. This community is that of the ultra-Orthodox Jews in Israel.

This chapter will focus on the events that have led to the current situation in Israel, which, as previously mentioned, has brought Israel, just recently, to bring three election campaigns without results and has limited the country's ability to form a government. This subject is an important topic to discuss and has caused a significant division in Israeli society today.

The ultra-Orthodox community votes for the Knesset to prevent its community members from serving in the military. There are two significant reasons for this. The first has been mentioned earlier in this book. The second reason is to sustain their unique lifestyle, education, and safety by obtaining particular budgets from the State of Israel. Although this community opposes the Zionist ideology, they will vote representatives into the Zionist institution of the Knesset and use their political leverage to keep members of the community from having to take part in Zionist acts (such as serving in the military).

Sounds confusing? For the Israelis, it's just reality. However, let me offer some clarification about this topic before moving on. There have been many religious men who have served in the military since the IDF's foundation. In the fascinating Jewish world of religion, there are vast numbers of opinions, ideologies, and disputes between groups. Coming from the secular world to Messianic Judaism, I can speak about external facts and outcomes, bringing these realities and insights into how things work inside these communities.

To be Jewish is to understand how other Jews think, regardless of what community they come from. Many religious men have served and have even had military careers, reaching high-ranking positions. Most of these men are religious Zionists, considered to be traitors to the "genuine" Jewish lifestyle in ultra-Orthodox eyes.

Let us start with some simple questions. Why is it that Israel can tolerate the exemption of thousands of young men from joining and serving in the IDF? What are the events that have led Israel to this reality?

The State of Israel's reestablishment, after 2,000 years of exile, came into existence following a chain of persecution throughout the lives of the Jewish communities in the Diaspora. The Holocaust was a pinpoint event that caused the rise of Zionism to be recognized, becoming the Jewish world-leading movement that brought the Jews to a state of their own. On May 14, 1948, Israel declared independence following the UN resolution that occurred on November 29, 1947. However, most of the world's leaders beseeched David Ben-Gurion, the first Prime Minister of Israel, not to declare Israel's independence.

In 1948, there were only 600,000 Jewish people in the land. That number included women, children, and the elderly. Ben-Gurion, an honored representative of the people, eventually declared Israel's independence for justified reasons and put the destiny of the Jewish people into the people's own hands. There was not much choice, since the British forces had already left the land. There is much to be shared about Israel's pre-establishment and early days in the coming chapter.

Throughout the struggle for Israel's survival, Ben-Gurion, as prime minister, agreed with the ultra-Orthodox community representatives that he would exempt Talmudic students from military service. He signed that agreement not realizing that doing so would become one of the biggest mistakes in Israel's history. The agreement came about after Ben-Gurion realized that the Nazis had exterminated most of the ultra-Orthodox communities in Europe. He presumed it was essential to keeping the heritage of Judaism. The exempted individuals were to supervise and monitor kosher foods, conduct religious rituals such as weddings and funerals, and perform circumcisions. This exemption was given to 400 men who were devoted to their studies, and was intended only for men that had chosen a rabbinical career. However, because Ben-Gurion forgot to limit the number of exempted men, this agreement has brought about unrealistic results. Because of this agreement, over 60,000 men have been permanently exempted from military service. No wonder this agreement has caused a division in Israeli society that persists to the present day.

Ten years later, in 1958, another arrangement came into existence. Back in the day, Shimon Peres was the general manager of the defense minister's office and had reached a more detailed agreement with the ultra-Orthodox community regarding how the exemptions should work. Ben-Gurion realized he had made a big mistake. In an official letter sent to one prominent rabbi, he wrote:

We are dealing with the moral issue! How come a son of one mother would die defending his motherland while a son of another mother would sit safely in his room studying? How could that be, while most of Israel's young men are risking their lives daily?

However, nothing changed.

In 1970, the exemption limit was removed. In 1975, the Supreme Court restored it to 800 Talmudic students a year. This decision did not last long because, just two years later, in 1977, the land experienced a political turnover. The Likud Party, led by a very charismatic leader, Menachem Begin, won the elections and became the ruling party.

The ultra-Orthodox parties, known for their right-wing ideology, gladly joined the coalition that was forming. The arrangements for the coalition partnership brought them their most desired result: removing the limit on the number of exemptions. Following their realization that, without the ultra-Orthodox parties as part of the coalition, the government would be too "narrow," the parties pressured the new prime minister to expand the circle of all exemptions. For example, it became enough for young women not to join the IDF simply by filing a certificate declaring that they were religious.

In 1986, the *Likud* party did not win enough votes to form a coalition with the smaller conservative parties, so created a national unity government with the second-biggest party, Emmet, led by Shimon Peres. The prime minister agreed to take office for two years for each party, in rotation. When Shimon Peres was the prime minister, he took steps to restore the Supreme Court's decision of 1975, albeit without success. In 1998, the Supreme Court ruled that Ben-Gurion's 1958 arrangements were illegal. The Supreme Court ruled that Knesset had to pass a law to resolve this matter within a year of the ruling. In the same year, 1998, the Tal Committee, named after its supervisor, Judge Tzvi Tal, was assigned to research, write, and submit a report that would offer conclusions and solutions. In April 2000, the committee published a detailed description and with answers to how to integrate the Orthodox Jews into the working circle, removing most of the exemptions from service in the military. One of the committee members, Rabbi Asher Tenenbaum, refused to sign the report. Following this committee's conclusions, the Knesset proposed a law that was passed by 51 to 41 votes.

The law that the Knesset passed contained the following guidelines:

1. *Yeshiva* students (Talmudic rabbinical students) would be exempted from any military duty until the age of 22.
2. Once they reached 22, they would have to choose one of the following options,
   a. To return to the *Yeshiva*, after showing evidence that they had studied there,
   b. To join an employment field and serve the military for a full term (married men would serve for a shorter period, or,
   c. Join the national service for one-and-half years without an exemption.

However, the Supreme Court again nullified the law in 2012, claiming that it was not constitutional. This was odd, since Israel does not have a constitution! That is, although some consider the independence declaration to be Israel's constitution, there is no written constitution, like there is in the US. It's all very confusing, rejecting a law by claiming it is unconstitutional when no such document exists.

While the law did not affect "dead in the water" individuals between 2003 and 2010, the period did in fact see a 60% increase in exemptions. Here are some examples of the increases during these years: in 2003 there were 39,200 exemptions; 2005, 46,500 exemptions; 2007, 52,000 exemptions; and 2011, 54,000 exemptions.

In a country as small as Israel, with fewer than 8 million citizens, these kinds of numbers are highly critical. Since independence, Israel has endured seven regional wars, two internal wars with Palestinian terrorists, and several ongoing small-scale military operations, especially retaliation operations. The price Israel has paid, losing its youngest men and women to protect itself, is significant. There have been 24,000 people killed since the country's foundation. In Israel today, most citizens have experienced losing a loved one, whether a close family member, relative, or friend. The presence of a community of people who refuse to protect the land is causing a deep division among Israel's people. Avigdor Liberman, the head of the *Yisrael Beyteynu* (Israel Our Home) party, received eight seats in the Knesset by promising his voters that he would pass laws that would mean that the ultra-Orthodox community would be required to serve in the military, the same as most Israelis. Following two campaigns, he refused to join a coalition. Because of him, Israel had to go through a third election. This shows how deeply felt the division is between secular citizens and the ultra-Orthodox community today.

As described previously, the ultra-Orthodox world reveals many streams of Judaism, with many internal divisions. For example, the ultra-Orthodox Jews who originally came from North Africa, will not celebrate Passover with those who immigrated from Europe; this is due to divisions based on specific dietary laws observed during the Passover. That is, one part of the community has its own commentary about leavened food, about which the other is in total disagreement Further to this, there are also political divisions between the two segments of the community. The number of differences and internal wars among the various parts of the ultra-Orthodox community is tremendous. This subject alone might be an excellent source to write a book on—a very thick book! However, most of the anti-Zionist and anti-Israel actions flow from the European streams in the ultra-Orthodox world.

You might now ask yourself, does the refusal to join a draft military service make a community an enemy to its own country? After all, you might presume that this community simply wants to preserve its uniqueness, just like the Amish living in the US with their unique lifestyle.

Well, I wish that this presumption was the truth. Inside this community, there is a small but very influential group of ultra-Orthodox individuals that are so radical in their anti-Zionist ideology that some do not even carry an Israeli identification (ID) card. Some will not even use Israeli money, and they even fast or mourn on Israel's independence day. This small community, called *Neturei Karta* (a term derived from the Aramaic language, meaning "the City Keepers") engaged in anti-Zionist actions even before Israel's establishment as an independent state.

Rabbi Amram Blois was not considered to be the brightest rabbi in his community. However, his charisma and confrontational attitude made him the leader of this community, who was followed as an example. Born to a very zealous family under British rulership, then growing up in Jerusalem in the 19th century, he had no problem confronting the contemporary ultra-Orthodox community in Jerusalem regarding their internal issues. He considered Rabbi Kook, a Zionist rabbi, to be one of his fiercest enemies. Blois used to make a ragged doll of his opponent and burn it during demonstrations with his disciples. He led demonstrations against football games on the day of the Sabbath. During the independence war, in 1948, he walked with several of his disciples toward the Jordanians and requested that they grant him Jordanian citizenship. He claimed that the establishment of Israel as a state "is the work of Satan," repeating the words of his leader, the leader of the Satmar community, who was living abroad. Under Israel's sovereignty, Blois never used Israeli money, claiming it was filthy. He carried no ID certificates, as part of his defiance against the State of Israel.

Blois also used to fast on the Israeli day of independence and often excused the State of Israel for spilling the blood of the Arabs. He banned himself and his community from voting for the Knesset and called those who voted collaborators with the enemy. This was not an act of only one man; an entire community followed him during his lifetime. After he died in 1974, his followers regularly appeared in protests; they were especially against driving on the Sabbath in Jerusalem and in other locations in Israel. Although this is a small community, operating in Israel and abroad, they have an extremely well-funded monetary system for businesses, especially abroad. During the Palestinian uprising, they supported Palestinian terrorist families, claiming that they were the actual victims. They performed demonstrations against Israel and Zionism worldwide, while showing solidarity with the enemies of Israel. Also, during these demonstrations, they were often seen burning Israel's flag and praying for the land's destruction.

In 2006, the former President of the Islamic Republic of Iran, Mahmoud Ahmadinejad, officiated at a conference named "A World without Zionism." The goal of that conference was primarily to deny the Holocaust and form a coalition of countries against Israel. Several representatives from *Neturei Karta* were invited and warmly accepted by Ahmadinejad and the Iranians. During their meeting in his office in Tehran, they thanked him for standing up against the Zionists and calling them criminals. However, during the detestable conference, they repeated the ridiculous allegation that the Zionists had taken advantage of the Holocaust, collaborating with the Nazis to establish the State of Israel. It seems, therefore, that the President of the Palestinian Authority is not alone in his delusions.

During the Holocaust Memorial Day, a siren sounds all over the land to remember those who died. It is a sign of memory, grief, and respect. Most Israelis pause in their daily business and stand for that minute of remembrance. Even highway traffic stops, and drivers get out of their vehicles, standing and bowing their heads in memory of the victims. However, the ultra-Orthodox choose not to stand to honour the dead, even though many of their relatives were murdered during the Holocaust. Instead, some eye-witnesses have seen ultra-Orthodox individuals celebrating in national parks, especially during Memorial Day, regarding those who fought and were killed protecting Israel.

As a community, the ultra-Orthodox spend tens of millions of dollars trying to convert secular Israelis to their way of life. Many Israelis look for a life meaning, especially when they are released to civil life following military service. Most of them are not familiar with the ultra-Orthodox world, the community's opinions about Israel and Zionism, or their internal conflicts. For the Israelis, these people represent the true G-d of Israel, and they are the best of His chosen. Unfortunately, the reality is far from the truth. They are the offspring of a manufactured religion that interprets the Bible for their own needs, thinking they are doing G-d's will. In reality, they honor both deceased and living rabbis as gods, claiming that the rabbis' commentaries are more important than the word of G-d Himself!

Since most Jews in the world do not read the Bible as they should (i.e., from its source) they consider the ultra-Orthodox as the highest authority able to comment on the Word of G-d. Since the destruction of the Second Temple and the act of leaving it to the Diaspora, the priests have lost their authoritative position in the people's eyes. The Pharisees, who were the ancestors of the ultra-Orthodox community of today, led the people through their rabbinical order. By writing oral law commentary and sets of books guiding the Jewish lifestyle, officiating rituals such as weddings and funerals, and being present in community life, they assumed authority.

Amnon Yitzhak, an Israeli Rabbi traveling in Israel and converting secular Jews to ultra-Orthodox Judaism, has compared Binyamin Ze'ev Herzl to none other than Hitler. The reason for that claim is that Herzl, the founder of the modern Zionist movement, wrote in his journals that he wished to convert all the Jews to Catholicism. Yitzhak ignored the fact that Herzl eventually erased the remark from his diary, which he never published; additionally, Herzl was in fact being humorous. It is so unrealistic to believe that a young politician like Herzl, who tried his best to represent the Jews' vision of the land and often met hostile and cold opinions, could convert the Jews all at once, on a single Sunday. Most historians agree that Herzl was joking or making a political gesture to attract attention. However, Yitzhak, a man equipped with magnetic charisma and a sharp tongue, could not have cared less for this theory. He spread his opinion among his followers and listeners, which spread like fire among thorns. His goal was to destroy Herzl's good name; by so doing, he thought, he could beat the Zionist movement. Though this strategy is unrealistic, Yitzhak successfully converted a pretty impressive number of Israelis and Jews of various ages to *Haredi* (ultra-Orthodox) Judaism.

This Jewish Mission–oriented man undertook further actions that positioned him as an inside enemy of Israel. For example, he boycotted Knesset elections (although he campaigned once and failed), he often criticized the functioning of the IDF and its officers, and fiercely objected to joining the IDF.

Yitzhak, who came from a secular lifestyle and even served in the military before becoming *Haredi*, often beseeched women to dress humbly, completely cover their hair, and not drive a car. According to Yitzhak, women who operate a vehicle are not humble enough. His charm and reputation for performing miracles brought about conversions, even among many women, who adopted a rigorous *Haredi* lifestyle. By receiving contributions from wealthy Jews in Israel and across the world, he has become one of the most influential religious figures in this missionary field. However, he lives humbly with his wife and many children in Bnei Brak, a city mostly populated by ultra-Orthodox Jews.

On top of trying to push their way of life onto others, in some areas these Jews even use bullying methods to get their point across, causing uneasiness in a primarily secular public life. For example, some public bus lines are dominated mainly by the *Haredi* population, especially during rush hour when they are going to and from their workplaces. The ultra-Orthodox leaders have used their connections to convince the transportation corporation, EGED, to instruct its drivers to point women to the back of the bus, so as to not mix with the male passengers. Women who are dressed inappropriately could not travel. All these guidelines were utterly illegal; however, EGED followed them out of fear of the ultra-Orthodox community.

This terrible phenomenon was stopped by six courageous ladies who refused to move to the back of the bus, sending an appeal to the Supreme Court. One of those brave ladies was Tonya Rosenblatt. She sat at the front of the bus, which caused some men to attack her verbally. The attack involved curses and threats, but she refused to move from her seat. Later, after this unpleasant experience, she received several threats on her life, by phone and email and on Facebook. In addition, there were attempts to destroy her good name by saying that there were witnesses who would testify against Rosenblatt's promiscuous behavior. These witnesses said that Rosenblatt stood in the middle of the bus threatening to undress herself, which was a complete lie.

The courageous Rosenblatt decided, with a few other ladies, to appeal to the Supreme Court, which led to several public committees being called. These committees and the transportation minister, including the Prime Minister of Israel, rejected and decried the phenomenon. Although this all occurred in 2011, it still echoes today. Although the transportation company was instructed not to order their drivers to cooperate with ultra-Orthodox passengers' demands to force female travelers to the back of the bus, some passengers still tried to do so. A gentle request followed by a refusal would often lead to threats, curses, and even violence between travelers.

The facts presented before you are key facts that prove that this community is truly an enemy of Israel. Were someone to disagree with these facts, there are a few questions I would like to ask. First, why is it that none of the "main" ultra-Orthodox community has rebuked, banished, or boycotted the small *Neturei Karta* community? Let us put aside the argument about serving in the military for a moment. How can you, as a community, tolerate it when one of the fiercest enemies of Israel denies the Holocaust?

Second, do you not think it is hypocritical that, on the one hand, you oppose the Zionist movement but, on the other hand, take part in a Zionist institution, using your voting power to gain money and positions of control over the people? The ultra-Orthodox community accepts the benefits offered by the State of Israel, while being completely unwilling to shoulder any associated responsibilities. Who has given you the authority to dictate to people using threats, bullying, and blackmail? The questions presented here address just some of the issues that make this community an enemy inside the State of Israel.

If you would like to know about the structure of the ultra-Orthodox community in Israel and the Diaspora in more detail, I can recommend several experts' writing on this matter. The most eminent of these are by Prof. Yeshayahu Leibowitz (deceased) and Prof. Shlomo Avineri. Very few people in Israel and the Diaspora know as much about this fascinating world.

To understand more about the animosity between the ultra-Orthodox community and Zionism, read on to the next chapter. To gain this understanding, and much more about Israel's situation today, we must go back in time, 200 years before Israel's establishment. Many events and reformations have happened in the Jewish world, particularly in Europe, that have affected the Jewish world and Europe both.

Chapter 4
ON THE WAY BACK HOME

So, why is there so much animosity between the ultra-Orthodox community and the Zionist movement? Are you familiar with the story of Joseph and his brothers in the Bible? I think this story reflects how what happens in the past affects the present, although this story truly reflects another biblical story: that of Jesus and His flesh-and-blood brothers, the Jewish people. Until the 18th century, most Jews living in Europe were highly religious people, absolutely devoted to their community life. They lived in small towns called *shtetls*, working in small farming, tailoring, and Judaica craft, as well as studying rabbinical law. In these towns, the designated leader was the chief town rabbi. A rabbi was not just a spiritual leader. He was the town judge, a marriage counselor, the deciding arbitrator, and much more. His influence over the community was absolute.

For almost 1,800 years, the Jews lived with that kind of autonomy; however, Europe experienced several reforms during the Industrial Revolution of the 18th century: economic, academic, and cultural. Since the Jews were prohibited, during the feudal period, from owning land, one of their ways of making a living was to study for an academic profession. Do you want to know why there are so many Jews with occupations such as doctor, lawyer, or accountant? You will find the answer in that period in Europe. The Jews, trained to study rabbinical law from a very young age, were extremely skilled at studying. As a result, Jews went to universities all across Europe to attain higher education degrees, doing so at a faster pace than non-Jews.

The Europeans, upon becoming aware of this, made anti-Semite laws to limit the number of Jews that could register. However, the Jews would detach themselves from their place of birth, wander to another city, or even another country, in Europe to gain an education. This period in Jewish history is called the Period of Enlightenment, as it delivered the enlightened movement within the Jewish community.

The rabbinical rulership of its communities became aware of the changes occurring and showed hatred toward the forming of new movements. The emancipation that swept throughout Europe, and particularly Western Europe, resulted in the Jews becoming more and more involved in occupations fitting their education and even taking on government positions. It did not take long for these individuals to adopt Western clothing, shave their beards, and take on the lifestyle of the West, while retaining a more moderate Jewish lifestyle. In addition, there were cases in which Jews converted to Christianity because of their fellowship with the Christian community. That reality caused the rabbis to consider the Period of Enlightenment as an enemy of the Jewish people; as such, they did their best to block new ideas, adopting even more strict clothing laws and declaring some of the Jews in the movement outcasts.

As a reaction to these actions by the rabbis, the new movement's leaders established their own rabbinical order, one that fit their new modern ways. Out of this decision, the reformed and conservative Judaic denominations were formed. As with the story of Joseph, when the Bible shifts to the life Joseph was leading in Egypt, we need to focus on the events happening there; in our case, especially those events related to the enlightenment movement in Europe. The ultra-Orthodox rabbinical leadership rejected the growing trend, but gained enough popularity among the Jews to become the representatives of the Jewish people in the Diaspora.

Before focusing on the dramatic events of the last 200 years, a fact needs to be presented and emphasized. Back in 1995, Shimon Peres declared that peace with the Palestinians was the most extraordinary event of the last hundred years. Benjamin Netanyahu, the then-opposition leader, responded to these words by saying: "The greatest event that has happened in the last century is the establishment of the State of Israel!"

Although Netanyahu was younger than Peres, and with less political experience, he was right. Human history shows that there has never been a nation like the Jewish nation. Have you ever seen a group of people taken out of their birthplace twice and eventually returned to the same place? The first time, they returned from exile after seventy years in Babylon. Then, the second time, they returned from all over the world, literally, after 2,000 years.

Mightier nations than the Jewish nation—the Babylonians, Assyrians, and many others—have been conquered and disappeared, mixing with others. The Jews have kept their faith, traditions, and community regardless of the circumstances they faced. I, as a Jewish man, am very proud and respectful of this. To be part of a nation that has such endurance and resilience is a source of inspiration.

A few years ago, while enduring a significant crisis in my life, I complained to my brother about my agony, pain, and disappointments. My brother, a quiet man by nature, listened without interrupting my long list of complaints. When I finally finished complaining, he just replied by saying, "You're going to make it."

"That's all you can say?" I replied in astonishment, expecting to get more encouragement.

"Yes," he replied shortly, as fit his character.

"Why do you think that I'm going to make it?" I asked.

My brother's answer was swift and life-changing. "Because you are a Jew, you're going to make it," he replied, then said no more.

I have no words to describe what happened to my heart at that very moment. That simple statement shook me to the core of my being and let my spirit rise above and beyond my sad circumstances. It was an answer that echoes in me even today, and I know I am part of a nation that has eternity in it. This nation carries a supernatural power that is beyond the understanding of common sense. I must admit that my brother's statement continues to resound in my heart; it is what led me to write this book.

With these facts in mind, we need to return and focus on the enlightenment movement and the changes in Europe that led the Jewish people to their destiny. The enlightenment movement, which reached its peak and greatest recognition throughout Europe around 1870, was active in Central, Eastern and Western Europe. It even reached Jews that were living in Islamic countries. That movement's goals were the preservation of Judaism and the Jewish people as a unique religion and community with rights, while at the same time revealing and exposing the community to the culture of the Western world, philosophy, Jewish-Hebrew literature, Hebrew media, and more. In addition, its proponents made a great effort to integrate their followers into contemporary society.

The movement played a significant part in modernizing the Jews of Eastern and Central Europe, moving them from the little *shtetls* to the big cities, to universities, to the circles of the academic world, and even to the rings of European politics. Several names to recognize in this influential movement are those of Rabbi Baruch Schick, Yehuda Halevi Horwitz, Raphael Levy, Rabbi Shlomo Chalma, Marcus Herz, and Yitzchak Eisele. The most prominent figure, at the heart of the movement, was Moshe Mendelson, who was considered the movement's flagship. Mendelson was born in Germany, and, during his childhood, his Rabbi teachers noticed his brilliance and assigned him to rabbinical study. However, destiny chose a different direction for this bright young man. It took him a relatively short time for him to become the preeminent leader of the movement, followed by Jews and even Christians. He taught himself German literature. He was also a very skilled business owner in the textile industry, which was the primary source of his wealth. In addition, he received prestige and medals of honor for the poems and essays he wrote.

Mendelson also received the status of *Schultz Jude* (Protected Jew) from the King of Germany. This status serves as awful proof of the level of anti-Semitism that was present throughout Europe and in Germany specifically. The enlightenment movement led to more dramatic events and changes for the Jews in Europe, starting in France.

Following the French Revolution, which occurred in 1789, and the transformation from feudalism to administrative rulership in France, there were more opinions about equality. Since the French Revolution started with the idea of equality, it was just natural to discuss the status of the Jews and how to integrate them into an equal society in France. In this way, friends moved to a new age with emancipation.

The concept and process of emancipation helped people, whether of low or high status, to become equal. Thus, the Jews, considered to be the weakest of any class (especially by several anti-Semite Christian theologians, who blamed them for rejecting Christ) suddenly became the center of discussion in French society in relation to equality.

In August 1789, the French people established their National Assembly. In that same year, they proposed a law for social equality. Two years later, in September 1791, the law passed, even though there was an anti-Semite objection within the assembly that claimed that the Jews did not deserve to be equal, despite the precepts of the Revolution. The anti-Semites' chief complaint was that the Jews were always praying to return to the land of Israel, and therefore, that their loyalty to France was questionable.

Can you believe that? Imagine treating American Jews whose vision is to go back to their land as traitors. It was an absurd accusation. There was a debate about whether Judaism was a nationality or a religion. An awkward reality then developed for the Jewish people of France. Emancipation was given to them, but they were required to prove their loyalty to France. The Jewish community showed signs of excitement, understanding that they were seeing an historic change in their status. They used their media to write poems and articles thanking the French people, raising funds to support the nation and encouraging their young people to join the

French military. That was the time for the enlightenment movement to escalate its power and influence throughout Europe, starting in France. In 1806, Napoleon invited honored members of the Jewish community to a conference, whose goal was to examine the loyalty of the French Jews to the nation. Napoleon wished to remove any obstacles from the path of the Jewish community in France and to integrate them into society completely. The honored members of the Jewish community declared their absolute loyalty to the French nation and its constitution. They also emphasized their commitment to harmonizing with the Jewish religion and objected to the accusations that the Jews were "a country inside a country."

Napoleon intended to reorganize the structure of the Jewish community to prevent the Jews from being accused of trying to form an autonomous community inside France. But, as we all say, a picture is worth 1,000 words. For example, there is a print showing Napoleon granting emancipation to the Jewish people. In that print, Napoleon, although shown as short in the figure, is portrayed as elevated above the Jews, who are bowing before him. The image also shows Jewish symbols, such as the menorah and the Ten Commandments, dumped onto the ground. It was clear from that print that the intentions of both Napoleon and the painter were to humiliate and subjugate the Jewish people, rather than sincerely welcoming them into French society.

The Jews of France welcomed the conference. Unfortunately, however, that period saw the formation of a more modernized anti-Semite structure. Anti-Semite theologians had accused Jews throughout the Middle Ages, saying that they were bound to eternal suffering on earth because they had rejected Christ. The theologians and religious leaders had absolute control over the rulers and the people, moving them to act in various ways against the Jewish communities. When they lost control over the rulers of the new era, modern forms of anti-Semitism appeared. Previously, Jews had been accused of causing plagues and diseases, of blaspheming against God, and cursing Christians.

There is one more form of anti-Semitism to focus on before moving on to the modern form of anti-Semitism. That form has caused suffering and resulted in many Jewish people losing their lives. In fact, in some regions today, some people still believe that this accusation is the complete truth. This accusation was that of blood libel, which falsely claimed that Jews require the blood of a Christian boy to perform their religious rituals. The claim was made even more specific by saying that Jews need Christian blood to make unleavened bread for Passover.

These accusations appeared before and during the Middle Ages. That God commands the Jews not to murder and not drink blood (Leviticus 17:11) did not change the mob's minds. If a boy went missing during the Passover festival, the Jews were immediately accused, brutally murdered, and persecuted by mobs. The first documented blood libel was in 1149, in England. The body of a young boy was found in the forest. Those who found it claimed that the body was pierced in both hands and under its ribs. Another Christian man claimed to have seen several Jews carrying a covered body to the forest. He also claimed that he once heard from a converted Jew that the heads of the Jewish communities decide each year which people they will use to carry out this ritual for the Passover feast. The abovementioned converted Jew never testified, simply because he was not found in the city as the Christians claimed; however, the tale was enough to accuse the whole Jewish community. This first case brought hundreds of blood-libel accusations. Christians with a dispute with a Jewish person would then falsely accuse them of something and thereby get revenge.

Throughout these times, Jews were executed, usually by being burnt alive after being tortured. As mentioned earlier, in some regions, especially in the Arab world, some people believed that blood libels were a fact. However, in the new era, anti-Semitism shifted to a more modern accusation. Realizing that the enlightenment movement had integrated the Jewish people more fully into society, making them more influential in most of society's circles, including even in the political world, the anti-Semites came up with a modern accusation: that the Jews had a plan to control the world; specifically, the global economy.

It is worth noting that Adolf Hitler combined both forms of anti-Semitism in his race theory, which served as a dangerous weapon against the Jews. Hitler used this theory to justify murdering millions of Jews. The primary justification for those who supported Hitler was that Jews were globally uniting to control the world. According to the anti-Semite accusers, the Jews were networking across the entire world to gain control.

The Protocols of the Elders of Zion is an excellent example of modern anti-Semitism. It is a book formed from an essay written at the orders of the Russian czar by the Russian secret police. The book was a hoax, but quickly became a bestseller throughout the world. Henry Ford, the American car industrialist, even funded 500,000 copies, which were distributed throughout the US in the 1920s. It also became an educational book for children during the Nazi regime in Germany. The book is 100 pages long and was edited by Pavel A. Kroschwan, known as a militant anti-Semite. It was edited in St. Petersburg in 1903. According to the *Protocols*, the Jewish people, who were part of a secret society, arrived at a private meeting in

1897. In that meeting, they formed a plan to control the treasures of the world and the people. Their supposed methods were to corrupt morality, take advantage of resources, and cause friendly nations to fight each other, using the Freemasons to conduct the events.

The *Protocols*, to be more accurate, is not a book. It is a collection of twenty-four anti-Semite essays written by the the *Uchrene* (the secret police) that have been combined into a single volume. Some people still, to this day, believe that this fabricated literature is the absolute truth. Although several historians and journalists have proved that these documents are entirely false, in some regions across the world, this collection of essays represents truth. The influence of this fictitious book has affected nations.

After the first World War, many Germans believed that losing the war was the result of a communist/Jewish plot. The Nazis increased the *Protocols'* publication to the crowds to deepen the people's hatred toward the Jewish people. Following the establishment of the modern Israel, Arab countries' leaders claimed that the Jews in Israel were planning to establish a kingdom in the Middle East after destroying the Arab nations. They customarily broadcast TV programs that were based on the *Protocols*. Even Japan was affected by this combination of essays and other literature connected to the *Protocols*.

The Dreyfus Affair, a political/anti-Semite scandal that divided the French Republic between 1894 and 1906, is another example of this form of modern anti-Semitism. Alfred Dreyfus, a 35-year-old artillery officer of Jewish descent, was tried and convicted of treason in an unjust court procedure in which anti-Semitism was involved. He was sentenced to life for allegedly turning French military secrets over to the German Embassy.

Before being exiled to Devil's Island in French Guiana, Dreyfus was publicly humiliated in a military ceremony, his ranks and parts of his military uniform removed. He spent five years on the island. In 1896, an investigation by Georges Picquart, head of counterespionage, found a piece of fresh evidence connecting another officer, Ferdinand Walsin Esterhazy, to the case. High-ranking military officials reviewed the fresh evidence, then suppressed it. In a military court, which lasted for just two days, they acquitted Esterhazy, making additional charges against Dreyfus for forging documents while he was in exile.

Eventually, the fresh evidence reached the journalist Emile Zola, who wrote an open letter called "J'Accuse" in the *L'Aurore*. This letter garnered public support, and pressure was put on the government to reopen the case. As a result, Dreyfus returned to France in 1899 for another trial, finding a country much divided over the matter and exposing anti-Semite motives. Zola received death threats throughout the entire trial. In addition, Dreyfus' family experienced harassment from an anti-Semitic character, and several other Dreyfus supporters received threats.

The new trial resulted in another conviction and a ten-year sentence. This time, however, Dreyfus was pardoned and released. In 1906, Dreyfus was pardoned and reinstated as a major in the French Army. He served throughout the whole of the first World War, ending his service as a lieutenant colonel. He died in 1935.

The whole Dreyfus affair was an example of how much hatred toward the Jewish people was under the surface, even in France, a country that sought social equality for all.

In total, the emancipation process took 125 years. In imperialist Russia under the Czar, however, the Jews did not receive liberation. The Czar forced the Jews to settle in a particular area in Russia; only a tiny percentage of wealthy Jews could live in Moscow. After the assassination of Czar Alexander II, the Jews suffered pogroms and massacres that lasted until the first World War. This sad fact caused over 2 million Jews to immigrate between the years 1881 and 1914, mainly to the US. Only in the Russian October Revolution (1917) did the Czar grant emancipation to the Jews as one of his steps aimed at preventing the Bolshevik revolution. Thus, it took 125 years to emancipate the Jews of Europe, yet even then the Jews did not enjoy all the constitutional rights given to the rest of the citizens of Europe. Emancipation, from the Jewish perspective, had failed. This reality brought about the next idea that swept the Jewish world: Zionism.

Yiddish, the language developed by the Jews in Europe over 1,000 years ago, is a great communication tool between Jews throughout the world. It is a language whose sources are mainly German, with many Jewish/Hebraic concepts; for example, newspapers written in Yiddish use Hebrew words. Yiddish was a vital communication method between the Jews situated throughout Europe, especially during the new era and in the two world wars. For example, a Jewish man from a *shtetl* somewhere in Romania could travel to a big city like Paris in France, and without knowing a word of French, he could walk to any synagogue and communicate in Yiddish. It was and still is a unique language with which to communicate in daily life, media, and Talmudic study.

I remember, vividly, working as a photographer at ultra-Orthodox weddings, hearing tiny boys and girls speaking Yiddish to their parents. Most likely, none of them were born in Europe, nor even were their parents. However,

Yiddish is still alive and kicking. It is essential to mention this because this language and method of communication enlarged and increased the enlightenment movement to a level that eventually affected the birth of modern Israel. Yiddish was a great tool that helped transform ideas and knowledge and allowed Jews to get organized quickly.

The outcome of the enlightenment movement caused the Jewish people to be exposed to socialist ideas. In 1897, the Jews founded the first federation of working Jews, named "The Bund," in Lithuania. These kinds of Jewish organizations, amid the Industrial Revolution and the rising levels of anti-Semitism, gave birth to a new movement: Zionism. In addition, the shift in Europe's defining nations induced many Jews in Europe to revive the ideology and the desire of the Jews to return to Jerusalem: to Zion. The goal of Zionism was to return to the land, bring European culture to its settlers (Jews and Arabs), and revive the Hebrew language.

Undoubtedly, the figure most identified with the Zionist movement is Binyamin Ze'ev Herzl. Theodor Herzl (his European name), an Austro-Hungarian Jewish journalist, was born in Budapest, Hungary. His journalism led him to be involved in political activities. While he was analyzing the desire of the enlightenment movement for Jews to be equal citizens in Europe, Herzl proclaimed a different solution for the Jewish people. Believing that anti-Semitism was the main reason why the Jews were not equal citizens, he presumed that establishing a Jewish state in Israel would be the right step to stop this inequality.

So, in 1896, Herzl published a book called *Der Judenstaat* (*The State of the Jews*). In this book, he predicted the establishment of the State of Israel. One of his quotes is carved in the minds of millions of Israelis and Jews around the world: "If you desire it, it is not a legend." By this, he meant that if the Jewish people wanted to have a state, they would get one.

Herzl's book caused great excitement, especially among the Jews in Eastern Europe, who believed that they could duplicate socialist ideas in a new state in the Middle East. This reaction was the birth of the Zionist movement and its first meeting, called "The Zionist Congress." The first such congress happened on August 29, 1897, in Basel, Switzerland. After the meeting, Herzl was quoted as saying "In Basel, I have established the Jewish State."

Out of this congress, the Zionist world union came into formation. The ultra-Orthodox, naturally, opposed the movement, claiming that it was entirely secular. Herzl responded with a declaration that Zionism would harm no stream of Judaism. In parallel to that, the Bund, which supported a national revival and autonomy wherever the Jews dwelled in Europe, opposed the Zionist idea. By now, the Bund was supported by 2.5 million Jews and was a potent organization back in the day.

The demographic changes, economic developments, and rise of anti-Semitism in Europe led to a massive emigration of Jews from Eastern Europe, mainly to the United States of America and Britain. Other individuals, predominantly young Jewish men and women who were full of ideological thought and courage, emigrated to the land of Israel. The word for emigration in Hebrew is *aliyah* (going up, or rising). With that idea in their hearts, hundreds of immigrants came during the first phase of *aliyah*, which occurred between 1881 and 1904. The second phase, with 35,000 Jews, happened between 1905 and 1914. During the first World War, the number of Jews living in the Holy Land climbed to 85,000.

Although the Bund opposed the Zionist movement, many Jews from socialist backgrounds joined and supported Herzl. This has to be mentioned, because there were developments and divisions inside the Zionist movement that will be discussed later in this book.

There were five major immigration phases before the establishment of the independent state of Israel. During the whole phase of immigration to the land, Jews were purchasing land from Arab landholders. Though the Jews had the biblical right to their promised land by God, they recognized that it had to be redeemed through purchase. Most times, the Arabs sold hard, uncultivated parcels of land for more money than the land was worth. The previous owners were later amazed to see flourishing land in places where they had failed. The dedication of the Israeli pioneers and their desire to study agriculture manifested in the fact that what they bought saw results. Most land purchases were made by wealthy Jews that came to Israel often. Some even settled in the land, helping the growing Jewish community. These people are called "The Land Redeemers;" among them were Menachem Osishkin, Yehoshua Chankin, Moshe Montefiore, Edmond James de Rothschild and Shmuel Blum.

These immigration phases brought 600,000 Jews into the land of Israel in 1948. Following the establishment of Israel, the Zionist movement became the dominant movement among the Jewish people; this has been the case up to the present day.

It is essential to consider the streams within the Zionist movement itself. Most people interested in knowing more about Israel's history think that Zionism is one solid, undivided, one-goal movement. The truth is far from it. There are several streams and divisions in the movement itself that almost led to a civil war. It's pretty natural to know that there was a division. As a son of this nation, I have realized that there would be a hundred opinions if there were three Jewish people in one room discussing a single matter. The answer to the question "How many Jews are needed to paint one room?" would be "Ten Jews." Why? Simple: one holds the brush and paints while the other nine advise him on what to do. However, religious Jews will answer "Eleven Jews—one is painting while the other ten men gather for prayer in a *minyan* [the minimum number of Jews needed to perform a prayer service] for the worker." Division and the blending of minds are part of Jewish existence. My advice to you, if you decide to visit the land: do not bring a political topic to the table if you socialize with the locals, as they will argue with you until you're blue in the face!

The above division can be seen in Zionism. Right after the first congress, Zionism was divided into several streams, each of which saw itself as the leader of the whole movement. The first main stream was Socialist Zionism (the red Zionism that came out of communist Russia). The leaders of that stream were Yitzchak Ben Tzvi, Yoseph Brenner, David Ben-Gurion, Berl Katznelson, Chaim Arlozorov, and Nachman Sirkin, among others.

The other two streams that should be mentioned are Revisionist Zionism, established by Ze'ev Jabotinsky, and Religious Zionism, established by Yitzchak Yaacov Reines. There are several more streams in Zionism, such as Practical Zionism, Synthetic Zionism, Labor Zionism, Cultural Zionism, and Reform Zionism. However, the streams that formed the history of our nation, and brought Israel to its status as an independent country, are the first three streams mentioned: red; revisionist; and religious.

So that you can understand the divisions and Zionism itself, I need to share this story with you. Herzl, whose stream of Zionism was more political than ideological, offered to establish the new State of Israel in Uganda. All the other Zionist streams rejected him. In fact, after this suggestion, he lost much of his popularity in the movement, for that reason and others. Eventually, the race was between the Revisionist (blue and white) Zionist movement, and the Socialist (red) movement. This struggle was not just political and ideological; it eventually became vital to the existence of Israel's destiny. More on this in the coming chapter.

Chapter 5

RED VS BLUE-AND-WHITE ZIONISM

Although Theodor Herzl was the founder of modern Zionism, he was eventually rejected for offering his ideas. His life was relatively short, and he passed away at the age of 44. His contribution to the Zionist movement was tremendous. He was buried in Vienna, Austria, but his body was reinterred in Jerusalem, following Israel's independence. The burial site is called "Mt. Herzl." Most of Israel's previous prime ministers, presidents, and honored people are buried there as well.

History has shown that great people are recognized during a major reformation in society, while some people experience a glorified moment of fame and are eventually pushed aside. A great example of this is Naftali Herz Imber, a brilliant man and composer who wrote the *Hatikva*, the Israeli national anthem. Such a person should have been honored and respected, as he was part of the Zionist movement for much of his life. However, his decisions and attitude led him to die somewhere in the United States (US), without a penny, at the age of 53.

Imber's attitude was so bad that he was removed from a Zionist conference after arriving drunk. While he was being pushed out of the door, he commented, "You can kick me out, but my poem will remain with you forever." He was right. He was buried in the US; however, in 1953, his body was reinterred in Israel.

It is an undeniable fact that the Zionist movement's beginnings were quite rocky. However, things improved when the movement began to escalate its power among the Jewish people.

There are two major streams in Zionism to focus on regarding their contributions to the establishment of Israel: the Socialist (red) Zionism, and the Revisionist (blue and white) Zionist movement. Although they had their differences, these groups moved toward establishing a Jewish State thanks to one person that bridged the two: Chaim Weizmann. Weizmann came from the world of biochemistry, and was highly respected by the British government for developing a restorative material that helped manufacture cordite explosives during the first World War. This chemical breakthrough allowed Weizmann to meet top British officials to discuss Zionist matters.

Although Weizmann was the founder of another stream of Zionism (Synthetic Zionism), he reconciled the two major streams, thereby moving the cart toward its goal. His diplomatic efforts among the British officials brought results. After meeting several officials, including Winston Churchill, he met a person whom many historians and Zionists worldwide consider to be the cornerstone of the design and fulfilment of the dream of a nation for the Jewish people. This man's name was Sir Arthur James Balfour. Balfor was the British official who wrote the declaration that was later called "Balfour's declaration." Balfour, a previous Prime Minister of the United Kingdom (UK) and the foreign secretary when he was writing the declaration, issued this vital document on November 2, 1917. It took the form of an open letter addressed to Rothschild, who was the British Jewish community leader. The declaration offered support for the Jewish people's establishment of a Jewish home in the land of Israel. The Jewish community received this declaration with gladness, comparing it to the declaration of the biblical Cyrus. However, the Arab world rejected it.

It is exciting and funny, sometimes, to see how destiny works. Here is a great historical example: Chaim Weizmann did his best to meet British officials and politicians, with the aim of representing Zionism to them in person. Eventually, he held a lecture that Balfour attended. During the lecturer's Q&A session, Balfour asked Weizmann why the Jews objected to settling in Uganda. Weizmann replied by asking, "Mr. Balfour, suppose that you get an offer to replace London with Paris. Would you agree?"

"But," Balfour replied to Weizmann, "London is ours!"

Weizmann, a very eloquent man, replied with much Jewish sarcasm, "You've told the truth. However, Jerusalem belonged to us while London was just a collection of swamps."

This was a brilliant, sarcastic remark from Weizmann, showing that historical changes may happen just because one person is present in the right place, saying the right words. Weizmann's contribution to science, his efforts to bridge the Zionist streams, and his diplomatic efforts made him the first President of Israel. He died in Rehovot, Israel, on November 9, 1952. The scientific institute in Rehovot (the same scientific institute where he developed the invention helping the British during the first World War) was renamed the "Weizmann Institute for Science" in memory and honor of his contributions to the nation.

So, why did Weizmann need to bridge between the socialist and revisionist movements? The answer to this question is because there were so many differences between the two that it took a more neutral man to move the movements' destiny onward.

The differences between the movements are significant—vital, in fact.

Let us start with the socialist movement, which was formed following the Russian Bolshevik revolution that influenced other nations in Eastern Europe and even countries in the Far East, such as Vietnam and China. The Eastern European Jews, inspired by the revolution and acknowledged as partakers of the Russian Revolution, the leadership, such as Trotsky, were eager to duplicate this social revolution in the land of their fathers. Their base was Marxist, which is the basis of the labor party in Israel that ruled from 1948 until 1977.

It is crucial to show that there were three major streams inside Socialist Zionism itself. The first was *Hapoel Hatzair* (the Young Laborer), founded by Aaron David Gordon, known more widely as A. D. Gordon. *Poalei Zion* (the Laborers of Zion) was the other stream, established by Dov Borochov and David Ben-Gurion. Later, the youth movement *Hanoar Haoved* (the Laboring Youth) came out of this stream. The third stream, *Hashomer Hatzair* (the Young Guard), was founded by Meir Yaari and Yaacov Chazan. The last stream mentioned was considered the most radical among the three streams, and held up the Soviet Union as the ideal society. In its view, the blood spilled during the communist revolution was an essential means of bringing the world into a utopian society.

The divisions among the streams were as follows:

1. Whether to speak Yiddish or revive the Hebrew language.

2. Whether to associate and be in full solidarity with the Soviet Union.

3. Whether to agree with the United Nation's partition plan (the *Hashomer Hatzair* stream did not want to agree with the plan and demanded more territory, while Ben-Gurion's stream agreed to it).

The following information that I will share with you about Socialist Zionism is mainly hidden and unrecognized by the Israeli public for political reasons. Prior to Israel's independence, the leaders of Socialist Zionism showed their opposition to the idea of Israel becoming independent. The party also acted against the Jewish religion itself. Although some historians disagree with this statement, it is tough to argue with historical facts; eventually, actions will speak louder than words. The best way to observe a person, organization, or movement is through its activities. During the presentation of events here, I will share further information about the revisionist stream so as to highlight the differences between the two major streams that have carved the reality in Israel today.

The outcome of Balfour's declaration, issued in 1917, was negative and unfriendly to Jewish emigration to the land.

To please the Arab world, and maintain diplomatic, economic, and social relationships for the benefit of the British Empire, they issued a set of bylaws and rules against Jewish immigration and Jewish settlers in the land. These collections of laws, bylaws, and regulations were unified into a book called the *White Book*, or *The White Paper*. At first, this book manifested and fulfilled the declaration by Balfour, the San Remo Committee, and the Treaty of Sevres. However, like many other politicians, the British operated with the principle, "in any move made, hide your deception." Winston Churchill, the writer of this set of laws, was considered the hero of the hour during the second World War. However, in his dealings with the Jewish people in the land, he was a great deceiver. He wrote these regulations in response to Arab complaints following their job losses. Therefore, Jewish immigration had to be limited, to help stabilize the economy in the land.

There is more to this set of laws that tried to put sticks into the wheels of the Zionist movement, especially in regards to immigration. This topic alone was supposed to unite the Zionists' stream, causing them to stand together against this decision and fight it. Did this happen? No. While Jabotinsky, the leader of the revisionist stream, opposed it, the socialist stream not only agreed to the terms but, using Weizmann's connections, approached the British authorities, suggesting that they would "monitor the quality of the Jews coming to the land," while respecting the annual limit imposed by British law. Once being delegated this right, the Jewish Agency received the authority to decide who could come to the land.

The results were horrific. The agency prioritized registered socialist Jews over Jews that were not taking part in the Socialist Zionism movement and deliberately barred religious Jews from Europe. They wished to create an artificial majority of Socialist Zionists in the land, while leaving most

Jews, especially those in Europe, behind. These days were the days of Nazi Germany, which was turning into Nazi Europe. There was already confirmed information about Jews in Poland being persecuted, beaten, killed, and thrown out of their homes. However, the socialists did nothing about it. Even Weizmann, who was supposed to be neutral and a reconciler for the cause, joined the socialists, declaring, "We don't need Jews from Nelski Street in the land of Israel."

Nelski Street was the main street in Warsaw, Poland, populated by primarily ultra-Orthodox Jews, which the agency considered one of its enemies. This decision cost the lives of hundreds of thousands of Jews, who were massacred by the Nazis and their helpers throughout Europe. The revisionists never stopped bringing Jews to the land, even when dealing with the British authorities was risky. Sadly, the Socialist Zionists criticized these efforts, calling them "illegal immigration" operations, all the while knowing that their brothers and sisters in Europe were being persecuted and butchered by the Nazis.

This may sound odd to too many, but Ben-Gurion and his partners in the Socialist Zionist movement objected to Israel's establishment as an independent nation. At the 17th conference of the Jewish Congress in 1931, Jabotinsky demanded a revision of and a focus on the Zionist movement to establish a Jewish State. In his reaction to the demand, Meir Yaari replied, "We boycott the idea of having a regime in the land. We will not oppress the Arab lives and workers in the land." Ben-Gurion also replied to Jabotinsky's demand, saying, "We will not agree to one national group controlling the other [meaning Jews controlling Arabs], not now, not in the future. Even if we have the upper hand demographically, we shall never do it!" Pretty shocking words to hear from the first Prime Minister of Israel, are they not?

"But," you may ask, "Why did Ben-Gurion eventually become Prime Minister?"

Good question! The reason for this is simple. After the British left, thanks to attacks by the underground organization *Etzel* (the National Military Organization) on the British forces, the Socialist Zionists (who were the majority) had no choice but to declare independence in 1948. The same Ben-Gurion as mentioned above spoke in front of the Peel Commission (a commission to investigate the reasons for the Arab revolt against the British) in 1937, saying:

> If we ever declare this place as a state, there must be only Jews in that state. Also, because of the complexity of the holy sites, we do not want to take the total responsibility for them; we recognize these places need to be under international forces' supervision, with the British mandate overseeing.

Ben-Gurion declared that he did not see Jerusalem as unified, nor as the capital of Israel. Sadly, the socialists brainwashed the public with their propaganda, suggesting that Ben-Gurion was the only person who could make Israel an independent state. This was not even half of the truth.

Did the Socialist Zionists, the ancestors of the radicals left in Israel, ever turn in people from the revisionist stream to their enemy? Sure they did! Do you remember the *Hashomer Hatzair* radical stream? In 1917, during the Ottoman rule of the land, the stream's members guided the Turkish intelligence to Jews who were members of an underground organization called *Nili*. This small group helped the British take control of the land of Israel from the Turkish empire. Since the *Hashomer* members were radical socialists who opposed the British, they had no problem turning in their people (*Nili*'s members were all Jews) to the Turkish oppressors. Two of them were sent to Damascus for trial and were executed by hanging, while the rest were imprisoned for a long time. The revisionists never committed such a treacherous act as this one by the socialists. Menachem Begin, the successor of Jabotinsky and the leader of the *Beitar* movement and the commander of *Etzel*, used to say, "Have mercy on the Ax that is thrown at you from your brothers."

The following historical event shows that the Socialist Zionists, as their Bolshevik ancestors did, would do everything in their power to destroy their opponents and remain in force, no matter the cost.

In the summer of 1933, Chaim Arlozorov, Head of the Political Department in the Jewish Agency, was murdered while taking an evening walk with his wife on the sandy beaches of Tel Aviv.

Ben-Gurion, who was visiting Warsaw, Poland, at the time, was informed and replied with a telegram that demanded the revisionists be accussed of the murder. All of that, without even seeing any evidence! Arlozorov's widow claimed that night, in front of Sergeant Freedman, a police officer, that the shooter had an Arabic appearance and that she heard the two men following them speaking Arabic before the shooting.

However, the socialists ignored her testimony, instead reprogramming her to point out a person who had nothing to do with his Arabic/Middle Eastern appearance, claiming that he was her husband's shooter. This crisis gave ammunition to the propaganda tool with which the socialists controlled the Jewish population in those years. The socialists also convinced the authorities to arrest any revisionist known to be investigated by the British Police.

Avraham Stavsky, the person who Arlozorov's widow pointed at, was convicted but later acquitted, thanks to the timely intervention of Rabbi

Abraham Cook, who claimed that relying on one person's testimony to convict a person is not justifiable.

One of the saddest facts about the whole murder case was that a professor named Dov Sedan, a Socialist Zionist, saw Stavsky in Jerusalem on the evening of the murder itself. He saw Stavsky at 7 p.m., while the murder occurred at 8 p.m. in Tel Aviv. Back in those days, it took three hours to travel from Jerusalem to Tel Aviv. Therefore, it was entirely out of the question that Stavsky could have murdered Arlozorov. Sedan remained quiet due to his socialist membership. Eventually, at the end of his life, he confessed, during a TV interview, that he was silent about this matter simply because he was a member of the red party.

The murder of Arlozorov is still considered a mystery. It might be the case that it was a failed robbery leading to a murder, according to Arlozorov's wife's description. However, the Socialist Zionists used this crisis wisely, using it to finalize their control over the Jewish colonies before they established the modern Israel.

The Socialist Zionists took many more actions against their opponents and against the people themselves. This subject alone is a topic that has enough material and historical data to fit ten solid hours of lectures. An unfortunate case showing the heartless behavior of the red Zionists occurred in 1942, when a group of 650 children arrived in Israel from Tehran, Iran. They were not Iranian children, but children smuggled from Nazi Europe by their parents, who the Nazis probably murdered while these children were still on their journey to the land. According to the children and smuggler's story, they walked for miles through forests and across mountain creeks, crossing desolated territories until they reached Tehran and, from there, came to Israel. It is so difficult to imagine the parents, knowing that they were going to die, sending their children to a place that they had never seen before, and acknowledging that they would not see them anymore. This was an act of despair and bravery by the children's parents. All the children in that group were Jews, little children who grew up in ultra-Orthodox homes. Since the socialists were in charge of immigration, which authority was given to them by the British, they sent the children to various places and settlements in the land. The children were orphans, with no known relatives in Israel; therefore, that seemed, in the socialists' eyes, the best solution.

The news about the *Haredi* children reached the ears of the ultra-Orthodox community, which felt the need to take care of these orphans. Those days were the days before independent Israel, at which time the ultra-Orthodox community had no power nor any political footholds in the land, nor any significant connections with the British rulers like the Socialist Zionists had.

The ultra-Orthodox delegation met with red Zionist leaders such as Ben-Gurion, Golda Meir, and Berl Katznelson, among others. The community's representatives spoke Yiddish to the reds, hoping to reach their Jewish hearts and somehow cause them to change their minds about the decision to separate the children. The community's delegation named families that would adopt all the children, some of whom did not have any children and hoped to adopt a child they could love and care for. Nothing helped: the red Zionists did not change their minds. They removed any Jewish symbols from the children, such as their sideburns, head coverings, and clothes, and sent them to the widespread settlements and kibbutzes (a socialist type of settlement) all over the land.

This painful history caused the Social Zionists to be branded as the enemy of the people of Israel. The revisionists had never oppressed the practice of religion; once they came into power in 1977, when Begin was the Prime Minister, the ultra-Orthodox communities flourished.

One more horrible story, an historical event, has to be added. Because of a decision by one man—Begin, the leader of the *Etzel*—a bloody civil war nearly occurred in Israel. When Israel was very young, a civil war would probably have meant that it ceased to exist; at the very least, Israel would not be as vital in as many areas as it is today. This historical event has been intentionally pushed aside by Israeli media for many reasons, notably their adoration of the left side of Israeli politics. There was no one else to blame but the ruling Socialist Zionists during Ben-Gurion's time as prime minister. This event is called "the Altalena Affair," after the ship that was the center of the event.

Before focusing on the Altalena Affair, it is worth noting some of the events that followed, especially those related to the British control of the land, which was about to end. An infrequent historic event occurred in the Holy Land. Usually, across human history, once an underground party has revolted against a colonial ruler and overtakes a territory, that party naturally becomes the ruling party or the newly formed government. In Israel, this was not so. With the help of the Israeli liberation fighters *Lechi* (Lochamei Cheirut Israel), the underground organization *Etzel* drove the British out of the land. Etzel was a more extensive organization than Lechi. Many in the Jewish settlements supported it, following the charismatic, humble, and determined leadership of none other than Begin, the beloved disciple of Jabotinsky.

Highlights of the operations against the British are as follows. On September 24, 1944, 150 Etzel members attacked four British police stations simultaneously, killing many British officers. On November 1, 1945, two

British soldiers were shot on a train, and five train engines were destroyed. February 25, 1946 saw a combined Etzel and Lechi force attack three British airports; twenty-nine airplanes were destroyed. On January 12, 1947, four British officers were killed by a bomb at the British government headquarters.

Some attacks were explicitly carried out by the Lechi organization, like the one on the King David Hotel in Jerusalem. This attack, which happened on July 22, 1946, resulted in ninety-one casualties, many of whom were British civilians. Since Etzel opposed attacks on British civilian targets, it did not take part in that attack. These attacks resulted in the British leaving the land in the night of May 14–15, 1948. Though the Etzel organization was the leading organization that ran the British out of the land, the red Zionists declared independence, founing the land's military out of their organization, called Hagana (the defense). But why did they do so? As mentioned before, it is unusual to see that kind of government standing firm.

The main reason why the socialists took control was that they were already a well-recognized institution, both locally and internationally. The second reason was that most of the settlements coming from socialist countries supported the Socialist Zionists. In addition, Etzel and Lechi were considered by some to be too radical and overly bloodthirsty.

On the day of independence, the socialists were those who declared independence. The first Knesset assembly took place in Tel Aviv City, since some of Jerusalem's parts of the city, the ancient and the eastern quarters, were occupied by the Jordanians. Though the Etzel and the Lechi joined in with the Hagana to build the IDF, the Etzel portrayed itself as the organization whose responsibility it was to protect the Jewish quarter and the Jewish community in Jerusalem. Therefore, there was an awkward situation in the first years of the young Israel: one united nation with two different military forces. This was a reality that the socialists would not tolerate, following their utmost desire for absolute control. It was simply a matter of time before a crisis would erupt.

And erupt it did. Since the Etzel needed weapons and supplies to maintain their protection of the Jewish civilians in Jerusalem, they needed supplies to protect Jerusalem. Therefore, the Etzel members used the Altalena to bring essential weapons, ammunition, and equipment from several countries in Europe. During their visits to these countries, the Etzel members contacted several Jews who wanted to immigrate to Israel. Back in those days, any vehicle might be used to transport Jewish people from Europe to Israel, even a ship loaded with ammunition and explosives. Though the days of Nazi Europe were over, the Jews were still in danger from aggression by local citizen. Therefore, Etzel brought 940 Jewish immigrants on board the

Altalena, a ship purchased in 1947. Israel was a very young country; the ship arrived at the shores of the settlement Kfar Vitkin on June 20, 1948, whereupon the crew started to unload the ammunition and the passengers.

Etzel notified the Israeli government about the ship's arrival. However, after unloading the immigrants, an Israeli military unit, routed from the *Hagana* and commanded by Dan Evan, demanded the Etzel men turn over all the weapons and equipment. Upon the Etzel members' refusal, the unit opened fire on the ship early on the morning of June 21. The Etzel members returned fire. In the ensuing battle, four Etzel members and two IDF soldiers were killed.

The ship then retreated to the sea and headed toward Tel Aviv, hoping to unload on its shores. No negotiations or attempts to negotiate were made. Instead, several military units were sent by Ben-Gurion with specific instructions to destroy the ship at all costs. The Etzel members on the shore were shot at; some were killed and some injured. Next, a missile unit, commanded by none other than Yitzchak Rabin (who would later become the Israeli prime minister), launched a missile toward the ship while people were still on board. The missile launch and heavy submachine fire caused the Altalena to catch on fire. Miraculously, it did not explode.

Several Etzel members jumped off the ship and swam to shore to save themselves. However, some witnesses claimed that the forces on the beach were shooting at the swimmers as well. Throughout the hellish rain of fire, someone yelled that Begin was on board, and attempted to stop the shooting. Begin came on board at Kfar Vitkin while the immigrants were going down to the shore. The claim of his presence was found to be valid; upon hearing that, the forces increased their fire, hoping to detonate the explosives on the ship and thereby kill Begin. Begin, who would later become prime minister, was not injured, but sixteen men from Etzel died during the shooting, some on the shore and some on the ship itself.

This event resulted in further tension between the camps. It was followed by Arlozorov's murder and rumors among the red Zionists that the Etzel was preparing for a revolution. The reds spread nothing but lies, proved by Begin's response to this event. If Etzel had indeed planned a revolution, this event would have been the trigger. Instead, Begin took the high road, commanding his forces not to respond to the massacre. He declared that there would be no civil war between brethren in the land. This decision by him was had a crucial impact on Israel's destiny. If a civil war had happened in Israel while it was so young and weak, it would probably have ceased to exist; at the very least, it would not be as strong a nation as it is today.

Without a doubt, Begin's decision made the Israel of today that many, including me, are very proud of. However, his decision not to fight brought him to a shallow point in his political life. It took him thirty years to win the elections, following which he became a leader that brought change to Israel's 1977 elections. During his time as prime minister, he signed a peace agreement with Egypt. Later, following terrorist attacks against Israel's northern border, he launched an operation in Lebanon that turned into a bloody war. He resigned from his position as prime minister following the events of that war and kept himself out of public life and away from media exposure until he passed away on March 9,1992.

The Altalena Affair is still a subject of debate among Israelis and historians. It is the highlight of the red Zionists' attempts to destroy the revisionists and gain absolute control over Israel, following the Bolshevik pattern. It is proof for our generation and generations to come that Social Zionism cares little about the people and is concerned only about one thing: rule and control. Eventually, the people recognized the reds' true colors, electing the party whose members fought to bring modern Israel to life.

Did the revisionists governing Israel through the *Likud* party make mistakes? Absolutely! However, they never oppressed the people as the Red Zionists did, never oppressed the Jewish religion, and truly liberated the Jews, understanding what true Zionism was all about. The sad fact is that there are still people who believe that Social Zionism's actions against innocent immigrants, who were coming mainly from Arab countries, as well as against religion and their political competitors, were essential to Israel's successful independence. This mindset is social propaganda at its best. Millions of people were persecuted and killed in the Soviet Union with the same excuse; that is, the success of the Russian Revolution. The Social Zionists were great disciples of this doctrine. Therefore, they sadly were, through their ideology and actions, an enemy within Israel.

The next chapter will focus on a minority group living in Israel. This group does not oppose Israel from an ideological, national, or religious point of view, even though their members are mostly Muslim. However, their often-illegal actions have resulted in the need for increased security and sleepless nights for those in charge of Israeli citizens' safety. Discussing this specific minority community is somewhat conflicting, since many of its members have contributed a great deal to Israel's security; even today, members of this community serve in the IDF. However, this community must be discussed, because of the damage caused to many Israelis who live in their area. This community is that of the Bedouins.

Chapter 6
"SONS OF SHEM"

The Bedouin community's issues with Israel are very complex. Israel has experienced outstanding contributions from this small community, which represents 3.5% of the population. As a person who has always been curious about this community since my childhood, my impression is that the Bedouin community is experiencing extreme polarities. On the one hand, the older generation, following a strict social code, is loyal to the Israeli state. Loyalty is translated into joining the Israeli Defence Force (IDF) and serving as high-ranking officers. On the other hand, however, the current generation shows signs of resentment and disloyalty to the state of Israel.

Some of the previous generation have been decorated with commendations for their acts of courage and heroism during various battles. The following are some names that are connected to success and fame in their community:

- Hassan Al-Hiab, IDF commander of the tracker patrol. He has achieved the rank of colonel, was revered by his commanders, and has been decorated three times for his command in battle and for saving his soldiers' lives.

- Amos Yarkoni, commander of the legendary "Shacked Patrol Unit." He received three commendations and one decoration called "Excellent Example," which is the third-highest-ranking decoration given personally by the IDF Chief of Staff in an official ceremony.

- Ismaeel Chaldi, the first Bedouin diplomat.

- Muhammed Ckaabia, a community activist and a recognized public speaker who promotes Israel worldwide.

- Ismaeel Abu Saad, Head of the Education Department at the Ben-Gurion University, Be'er Sheva, Israel.

There are also women, elevated from this community, on this honored list: Amira Al Hiab, the first IDF female fighter, and Rania Ukabi, the first Bedouin gynecologist in Israel. The list is long and impressive.

However, the other side of this community, sadly, is harmful. The results of the social structure within Bedouin families, clans, and tribes, which will be explained, are alarming. The social uniqueness of strict family esteem, polygamy, and pride has led some of the younger generations of the Bedouin community to commit crimes that often jeopardize Israel's security.

Before going into detail, I need to share a personal story with you. During my high-school years, we went on a three-day field trip, traveling to the southern part of Israel. On one of our visits, we were guests at a Bedouin tent. We experienced Bedouin hospitality, which involved being served coffee, tea, and a traditional Bedouin meal. The Bedouin people are known for being very hospitable. They have fascinating customs, rituals, and special foods that they offer when entertaining a guest. We heard a lecture from a local Bedouin dressed in his traditional Bedouin costume during our time in the tent. After the lecture, during the Q&A session, someone asked the speaker, "Isn't it time for all of you to move to the city and leave the tents? How can you raise children in an environment without electricity, running water, while rain drips through the tent?"

I thought that the young man who asked was vulgar. However, the reaction of the speaker affected me greatly. Raising his voice and pointing a finger upwards, the Bedouin speaker said, "The roof of this tent is made of camel's hair! During the winter, not one drop will come into the tent!"

The Bedouin speaker was upset by the question, flushing with anger and raising his voice. When he finished his answer, there was absolute quiet. You could hear a needle drop on the floor (or, to be more accurate, hear a needle falling on the tent's rug). I believe that everyone in the tent felt as I felt, concluding that evening that the Bedouin people were incredibly proud and passionate about the way of life they had adopted centuries ago. The Bedouin have been mentioned by historians since the 2nd century, during the Roman Empire. During that period, they emigrated from the Saudi Arabian peninsula, and their lineage is Semite.

There is an ethnic division among them: some claim to be the direct descendants of the biblical figure Joktan, son of Eber, the great-grandson of Arpachshad, who was the third son of the biblical figure Shem. Other tribes and clans proclaim they are direct descendants of Ishmael, the son of Hagar. Another fact is that there is no blood connection between the Bedouin living in Galilee and the Bedouin dwelling in the Negev and Sinai deserts. They are separate clans and tribes. During the Ottoman rule in the land, the Turks helped the Bedouin to settle and taught them agriculture. Under the British mandate, the Bedouin were hired (by the British) to build roads and railways. The Bedouin are not fully nomads; rather, they are half nomads. That means they choose a place to dwell with their tents and even build a home there, using the rest of the land to raise their flock and cultivate the land for agricultural purposes. They prefer not to dwell in a city and have rejected offers from the government of Israel to move to a city that fits their needs.

During the independence war, many Bedouin immigrated to the Gaza strip, not because they feared the Jews, but because they wanted to avoid joining the Arab nations' military, which was fighting Israel. Throughout their history, there has been a pattern in the strategy they have used to gain control over their region. First, they have chosen and adapted to the desert as a defence strategy, isolating themselves from their opponents. Their second strategy has been to intimidate settlements near their area, causing the settlers to leave. They have done so by burning crops, stealing farmers' equipment and livestock, and more. Once the settlers left, the Bedouin invaded and took over the vacant property.

This behavioral pattern should be recognized since it highlights the following events after Israel's Independence. In 1953, Israel enacted a land law that aimed to designate land for Jewish settlements, natural reserves, and military training zones that use live ammunition. However, since most of the Bedouin tribes were gathering in a specific area between four major cities, the Israeli government designated that area as theirs. The main reason for that decision was safety; the aim was to avoid casualties while the IDF was training in the Negev area. Thus, that area is called "the safeguarded area."

During the Ottoman Empire, the Turks, understanding the tension within the Bedouin community and the fact that there would be tribal wars over territory, designated the whole Negev and the Judean desert as belonging to the Bedouin, with specific territorial borders. However, Israel was not sensitive enough to these issues and instead concentrated most of the Bedouin in a much smaller space. Wandering and shepherding near or inside military training zones was prohibited. It was also decided that if the tribe or an individual Bedouin claimed ownership over a piece of land, this land would not be returned to the original owner, who would instead be given compensation. Unfortunately, the prideful Bedouin reacted negatively to the new situation in which they found themselves.

I have great respect for this ancient people and for many of their ancient traditions and skills. They have a long and proud heritage and deserve a good place in Israeli society. However, some have allowed themselves to be used by the enemies of Israel to threaten its security.

Although the Israeli government tried to improve the Bedouins' lives by building the cities of Rahat and Tal Shava, this was a failure. The area has become too small for the total population, especially in terms of pasturing territory, causing fights between the tribes. In addition, the cities that were built lacked municipal services such as water, electricity, and sewerage. Since the schools were too far apart and the transportation from the Bedouin areas to schools was insufficient, the children lacked an education. As a result, many left the ancient shepherding profession, trying to find jobs in the surrounding Israeli cities. Sadly, however, many used another method to gain money more quickly: theft. Reports of witnesses showed the Bedouins were roaming in prohibited IDF training areas, dressed in IDF-colored jackets as a means of deception and stealing military equipment such as rifles, ammunition, optics, uniforms, and soldiers' items.

The actual damage caused to the IDF in this way has been calculated as millions of shekels every year. However, the economic damage is a secondary issue, as the most crucial challenge Israel is facing is to its security. There is no other nation in the world that has as many enemies as Israel. The relatively easy access from the Negev to the Gaza Strip means that the Bedouin, using their trackers' skills, have the opportunity to sell this equipment to a very bloodthirsty customer: the Hamas. This terrorist organization, which controls the Gaza strip, constantly needs supplies from outside. Unfortunately, the Bedouin are resilient and crafty enough to bring these army goods to the wrong hands.

Back in 1979, the Israelis returned the Sinai desert to the Egyptians as a result of the Israel–Egypt peace agreement, thereby separating a number of clans and tribes. These communities are still networking on both sides of the fence, and most of the network connections result in the smuggling of weapons, drugs, and ammunition. One of their methods is to use tame camels to cross the border independently, heading to predestined locations. There are other methods, such as the use of night-vision thermal equipment, all-terrain vehicles, and even tunnels.

The Bedouins on the Sinai Peninsula have the reputation of networking with the ruthless Sunni terrorist organizations Al-Qaeda and ISIS. These terrorist organizations are still settled in some areas of the desert, in pockets of resistance. They have attacked several locations in the Sinai desert, killing hundreds of innocent civilians. This is very alarming to the Israeli security forces. The connection of the existing Sinai–Negev Bedouin network with the global terrorist organization Hamas might lead to horrific results for

Israeli civilians. The Israeli forces are doing their best to protect this border, but it is 143 miles long, and they have to deal with a very crafty opponent that knows the desert like the palm of his hand.

Stealing weapons and military equipment and selling them to a sworn enemy of Israel has put some Bedouin in the position of enemies of the State of Israel. Therefore, what they are doing is an act of treason. Although they are Muslims, most of the Bedouins are not motivated to harm Israelis for ideological reasons; however, they are doing so indirectly, through social, economic, and educational causes.

There is another kind of theft that has to be mentioned. However, before focusing on it, we need to acknowledge another topic within Bedouin society: polygamy. Polygamy among the Bedouins is quite common and influences several issues in Israeli society. Like other Western societies in the world, Israel has made it illegal to have more than one wife. Since Israel is a Jewish state, the law has also focused on non-Jewish minorities in the land, Bedouins included. According to the written law, there are two reasons why a non-Jewish citizen may be married to more than one person at the same time. The first case is if a spouse cannot file for divorce or cannot agree to divorce due to mental sickness. The second case is where the spouse is missing and has not been found for seven years.

However, the Bedouins do not abide by this law since, as Muslims, they follow sharia law. Since Israel is a nation that offers free religious practice, it does not interfere in matters of religion. Instead, it allows the Bedouins to marry one official wife (who is registered as the wife in the state documentation), while ignoring second, third, and even fourth marriages, which are performed by an Islamic person who is ordained to officiate Muslim weddings.

From a Western point of view, most women in the world will not tolerate sharing their husbands with another women. However, in a Bedouin family, first wives will encourage their husbands to marry more wives. Why is that, you might ask? The answer is quite simple. Once the husband adds a younger wife to the family, the first wife becomes the household leader. That means fewer household chores for her such as cooking, cleaning, and taking care of the children. The younger wives will work hard taking care of their and even the first wife's children.

In most cases, the first wife's children inherit the majority of their father's property. This leads to the main problem and outcome of polygamy in Bedouin society: children that are born out of second, third, and even fourth marriages have all had their education neglected and even lack proper housing, while the children of the first wife enjoy better conditions. Thus arises a major social issue when the deprived youth turn to crime.

It is enough to look at the biblical story of Isaac and Ishmael to understand the jealousy, hatred, and feelings of rejection that this causes, which have led to horrific results that echo to this day. The young (primarily) men, knowing that they have no status within their own families, seek the resources that will allow them to acquire income and prestige in Bedouin society. Most of their sources of income involve crime. However, since they want to be supported by their community, they will commit a "justified crime."

Using the methods of their ancestors to intimidate their non-Bedouin neighbors—the Jewish farmers—they harass them by stealing and damaging farm vehicles and agricultural tools, burning fields, stealing livestock, and using other methods of intimidation. For example, several farmers have complained that young Bedouins will approach them and ask them to pay protection fees so that their property will not be damaged or stolen. If the farmers refuse to pay, the property is then stolen, damaged, or destroyed.

The 2018 annual combined police and internal security report shows an alarming picture of this specific crime, under the section "Agricultural Crimes in the Countryside." This 1,360-page report presents a circular diagram of the crimes committed in the Israeli countryside. It shows arson, the invasion of pastures and damage made to irrigation systems, as well as the theft of bulldozers, tractors, agricultural tools, produce, cattle, beehives and honey, and pesticides and fertilizers.

The report also shows how the police lack the power to enforce the law, which makes the Jewish farmers very frustrated when dealing with this challenge. Some farmers take their own and their property's safety into their own hands by hiring security companies, installing cameras, and using guard dogs. In 2007, a farmer shot two burglars, killing one (who was a Bedouin). Researching the event, the detectives realized that four burglars had been there that weekend; they had poisoned the guard dogs and broke into the sheep manager. The farmer approached the four burglars, realizing that they were armed with knives. The only protection was his handgun, which he used, injuring two, one of whom died.

The farmer claimed that this was not the first time he had experienced a burglary; it was, in fact, the second burglary in less than a month. This farmer's story is one of many stories told by farmers who have experienced these kinds of acts. Here, the outcome was fatal. Feuding culture among the Bedouins will make the farmer their target. This farmer then has to keep one eye behind his back for the rest of his life to protect himself and his family.

Feuding, or avenging death, is rooted deep inside the culture of the people of the desert. The feud does not stop when the life of the one who has killed a Bedouin family member has been taken; according to Bedouin traditions, a family member may avenge his relative's death up to the fifth subsequent generation. One tale tells us that a grandson whose grandfather was murdered took an oath to avenge him by killing the son of the murderer. One day, he walked into his clan leader's tent with a bloody knife, saying, "I have avenged the death of my grandfather that happened twenty-five years ago."

The oldest man, upon hearing the avenger, took a long sip from his cup of coffee and said: "My son, what was the reason for being in such a hurry to act?"

The only way to cancel blood vengeance is by a special ceremony performed by honored community members called *Suulha*. Before that specific ceremony is performed, which is attended by parties on both sides of the dispute, selected leaders will help both sides to agree on the terms. Usually, the family or the clan who has committed the crime will pay compensation to the victim's family; this might take the form of money, camels, or other valuable property.

Several more issues have caused the Bedouin community to put itself in a position whereby it harms Israel's security, both agriculturally and financially. However, this book has focused on the central issues. In summary, Israel has failed to show sensitivity to this unique community's needs for the reasons mentioned and more. As a proud tribal people, some have chosen to act for good by taking part in and bringing glory to our dynamic Israeli society. Sadly, however, most of the people in this community, especially the younger generation, have developed feelings of resentment. Some of the bitterness is directed against their culture, but most of it is against Israel itself. This leads to an unbroken cycle of crime, theft, and intimidation, followed by Israel's retaliation. Maybe, in the future, some issues will be resolved that will lead this community to a resolution that will benefit all.

The next chapter will focus on an Israeli institution that is an essential institution within Israel and in any other normal, functioning country. This institution promotes and fights for the purest form of justice in society. However, in Israel, this institution has gained enormous power through treachery. It has become so powerful that it is now intimidating Israel's democracy; thus, it has become an enemy of the state of Israel. This institution is the Israeli Supreme (or High Court) of Justice.

Chapter 7
THE TYRANNY OF THE ISRAELI SUPREME COURT

Justice and only justice you shall pursue, that you may live and possess the land which the Lord your God is giving you (Deuteronomy 16:20)

The above quotation from Deuteronomy is a powerful verse that is supposed to guide any court system, especially the Israeli court system. The Israeli High Court of Justice (IHCJ) has made significant decisions since the reestablishment of modern Israel. This chapter will focus on some of the critical decisions it has made that have resulted in actual harm to Israel.

First, some facts have to be mentioned to clarify the reader's understanding of the complexity of the IHCJ before focusing on the events, the court's decisions, and the cases' outcomes that have brought harm to much of the Israeli society currently suffering under the IHCJ's tyranny. In contrast to the United States (US) Supreme Court, whose highest goal is to protect and define the US Constitution, Israel, to this day, does not have a constitution. Through the Bill of Rights, the US Constitution protects all aspects of an individual's freedom, including freedom of speech, freedom of the press, and other issues.

This lack of a constitution is crucial, because it has permitted the tyranny of the IHCJ.

Most Israelis reading these lines would immediately comment by saying that the independence declaration that Prime Minister David Ben-Gurion signed is the Israeli Constitution. However, they are entirely wrong, because it is written in the independence declaration that the nation's honored council represents only a temporary government. The primary goal of the interim government was to designate, oversee, and sign an established constitution. The provisional government was given a specific period within which to issue the constitution document; this fact was also written in the declaration of independence. The deadline for doing so was October 1, 1948.

The designated honored members appointed Dr. Zerah Verhaftig as the head of the constitution committee. Dr. Verhaftig, a gifted scholar from the academic and rabbinical worlds, worked immediately on the holy task given to him. But again, in Israel, things always have to be changed following elections. The 1949 elections caused a disagreement inside the committee itself. The major dispute was the difficulties involved in forming a constitution due to Israel's unique character as both a Jewish and a democratic state. Even though most of the committee wanted to construct a constitution, the minority that was opposing the constitution was much more vocal, threatening apocalyptic events should the constitution come into existence.

One of the minority's claims was a very awkward one: namely, that having a constitution would be unfair to Jews living abroad, who might disagree with the context of the constitution established by the Jews in the land. Imagine if people opposed the US Constitution, claiming that having such a constitution might harm future Americans who were immigrating to the United States. The context that the constitution would be offensive to future-born US citizens, as they might disagree with it? It was such a ridiculous argument.

Eventually, sadly, Dr. Verhaftig accepted the opinion of the minority and passed it on to the temporary government, which received his recommendation that it was not to establish a constitution. However, after the elections, the same committee designated to form the constitution was tasked by the Knesset to suggest fundamental laws for the Knesset legislation. So far, the Knesset has legislated fourteen basic laws that might be part of a future constitution; most likely, however, this will never become a reality in Israel.

The significant decision not to have a constitution is one of the vital decisions leading to Israel's experience of tyranny under the IHCJ. Let me explain. The existing Israeli law is based on common law, which was in force under the Ottoman rule over the land (for 400 years) and under British rule. The Israeli law system is based primarily on judicial precedent. On May 14, 1948, a new legal entity called "the State of Israel" was recognized. As described above, the temporary government, which became the current Knesset, has since legislated laws without establishing a constitution.

There is another aspect to understanding the complexity of the legal reality in the State of Israel. Since 1948, Israel has had several regional wars. Thankfully, Israel has won all these wars—I cannot imagine what would have happened if it had lost one. The result of these wars is that Israel possesses territories such as the Judah and Samaria areas east of Jerusalem, also called the West Bank. The Gaza strip, south of the city of Ashkelon, was taken as well.

Though Israel became larger in terms of its territory and resources, it had problems; specifically, a refugee problem. Since Israel did not want to install its laws in the territories it had acquired, a civil administration branch, supervised by the IDF and other sources, was put in charge of the population. Following this, the IHCJ opposed the State of Israel, making court decisions that risked the security of Israel and the safety of the IDF soldiers and civilians. How it did so will be discussed later on in this chapter; suffice it to say that the IHCJ, over time, opened the door to all matter of disputes that developed between the State of Israel and the Palestinians in the territories.

There are many aspects to the disputes that have arisen from Israel's security and safety needs. Israel is a democratic country; it enjoys free elections, freedom of expression, religion, and the press, and the freedom to organize and take part in political or nonpolitical organizations. Like other free countries across the world, Israel, too, has separated the powers of government. The legislature is the purview of the Knesset, the executive authority belongs to the government and the judiciary, the latter of which holds independent judicial authority.

The democracy in Israel is a parliamentary democracy, meaning that the government has been formed by the Knesset. The Knesset may declare a government non-training proposal. If it gains a majority of the vote for that proposal, this will lead to the Knesset and new elections dispersing. In short, the government is not independent, but depends on the Knesset to function. Therefore, the separation of powers in Israel is less than that in other countries, such as the US.

It is essential to emphasize here that, although there is a separation of powers they are not equal in authority. In terms of the normal functions of governing, one authority has to be superior over another, with the judiciary the least powerful and non-independent. Having that order of superiority is very reasonable, since the Knesset is the body that the people elect. Therefore, the Knesset is superior to the government, which comes from the Knesset itself. The judiciary is the only authority that the people do not elect; therefore, it is required to be humbler.

This is the reality that exists in other countries in the world; however, it is not the reality that exists in Israel. The judiciary indeed has to be non-independent, not least to prevent corruption in the government. The judge is the only authority permitted to define the law and to make a judgment, and no government or Knesset members or lobbyists should interrupt or influence them. However, since the judiciary needs to be humbler, as it is not elected by the people, it is required not to interfere in political matters, and especially not in explosive issues.

In Israel's early days, the judiciary was well aware of this concept. For example, back in the early 1960s, Prime Minister David Ben-Gurion wanted to establish diplomatic relations with Germany (or, to be more accurate, with West Germany). Israel, back in the day, was a very young country, just twenty years old. Many people who were living in Israel were Holocaust survivors. Some of them had come to the land with nothing but their clothes. Many of them had lost their parents, brothers, sisters, and all their possessions. The idea of establishing diplomatic relations with a state who had been responsible for the murder of 6 million Jews was unbearable.

Ben-Gurion signed a severance agreement with the Germans to lose Jewish possessions during the Holocaust. That agreement caused a significant storm among the Holocaust survivors, who claimed that he had sold the memory of the murdered for money. The Holocaust survivors and their children (the latter of whom were affected by their parents' trauma) could not bear the fact that a German flag was raised above an embassy for all to see.

The IHCJ received an appeal to Ben-Gurion's decision that asked for the ICHJ to reverse it. The IHCJ responded to appealers by saying that the matter discussed was not *spieth*. However, understanding its place as the humbler authority, it decided not to interfere with the political issue that Ben-Gurion's government had created.

Several more decisions by the IHCJ proved this concept. In the 1980s, this concept faded, but the change was recognized. As mentioned earlier, as Israel owned territories whose population was without Israeli citizenship, some cases have required the IHCJ's interruption. The IHCJ, seeing itself as the defender of human rights everywhere, interrupted issues in such a way that it trampled and even wholly stopped the actions of the Israeli government. By doing so, the IHCJ became superior to the Israeli government.

The IHCJ is comprised of 15 justices, two of whom are registrars. The President of Israel appoints them after being nominated by the Israeli Judicial Selection Committee. Once selected, a judge serves until they reach the retirement age of 70 years old.

Before moving on to details of how it all happened, let me share a very recent event that occurred right after the third elections of 2020, as I believe this will allow you to understand the severity of the way in which the IHCJ controls even the Israeli parliament, the Knesset. During the election storm that Israel endured through three different election campaigns, the IHCJ demanded the replacement of the Knesset chairperson. Because Israel had a provisional government following the elections, the IHCJ accepted an appeal from several individuals and demanded that the Knesset chairperson, Yuli Edelstein, gather the Knesset to elect a new chairperson. Edelstein refused to do so. One reason for doing so was that it was unacceptable for the IHCJ to interfere in parliamentary affairs.

Edelstein was utterly right. However, immediately after his refusal, he was ordered again by the IHCJ to follow its demands. Eventually, Edelstein resigned without complying with the IHCJ.

This event has to be mentioned, since there has never been such a case recorded in any other democratic country. The people of the US, for example, will not tolerate any situation where their Supreme Court tries to influence or dictate any congressional activity or crisis, no matter how complicated it is. Unfortunately, however, the IHCJ has dared to do so. The decision it attempted to influence was minor compared to other issues that affect Israel's security and safety—for example, setting out borderlines and guarding the concrete walls to protect Israelis and Israeli settlements from terrorists or sniper attacks. This task is wholly given to the minister of defence, who uses their judgment and has the ultimate word. However, the IHCJ, accepting appeals from local Palestinians, ruled that the right thing to do was to stop the defence minister from doing what was best to protect their nation.

It is worth noting that most of these appeals are sponsored by organizations that have declared themselves as human rights organizations. In reality, these organizations are anti-Israeli organizations that believe that the best solution, for a better Middle East, is to remove Israel from the map. The IHCJ, knowing that fact, still has no problem cooperating with and turning against its own country, jeopardizing its security.

Let us now focus on the reasons why Israel finds itself in this terrible reality, with the IHCJ having so much control over the Knesset, the government, and the safety of so many lives in Israel. Here, it will be more accurate to focus on a specific person, rather than on a period of time. The name of the person is Aharon Barak, who was promoted to the position of IHCJ President. Barak has been an IHCJ judge since 1978. He was a Holocaust survivor, saved by Lithuanian farmers who hid him and his mother during the second World War.

After the war, he immigrated to Israel and served in the IDF. After his service, he went on to study law and became a judge. All of his immediate family were lawyers by profession. He has been accused of nepotism concerning his wife's promotion, and all of his children received desirable internships in the IHCJ court while he was a judge there. These accusations have had no results. His children continued their internships there and were even promoted to higher positions later on. During his IHCJ presidency, he started reforms that did not previously exist at IHCJ, which have made the IHCJ superior to the other authorities. He actively brought these reforms to pass, earning the title "the most activist judge in the world," making him the most dictatorial judge.

The first reform was to reverse the mindset: from "not *spieth*" to "every matter is justiciable." Barack ruled, in 1986, that any matter, regardless of whether it was a political issue or not, might be handled by the Court of Justice. He claimed that any action made by an individual, organization, or state could be defined and analyzed under the law. Up until his tenure, the IHCJ's main role was to resolve disputes between two or more sides. However, in his rulings, Barack said, "The main starting point of examining normative judgment is that the perception of the law is a system of prohibitions and permits any action to be permissible or prohibited in the legal world."

Israel had to play by the rules, even though the terrorists (for example) did not. There are many aspects to this topic alone. For example, Israeli intelligence captured a terrorist who was part of a terrorist group attacking a specific location in one of the Israeli cities. The only way to get information to prevent this evil act from that person was by force. This is not a hypothetical situation but has happened in Israel, many times. Barak said that the investigators might do something wrong to get intel, or, maybe, uncle is permitted now, but might be prohibited. This gives enormous power to the IHCJ, while the security authorities might lose their hearts doing the holy task of defending the Israeli people. Barack also states that "There is no action that the law doesn't apply. Their is no such thing as a 'legal vacuum.' Concerning this matter, there is no exception! Whether or not the action is political, a policy or not, any matter is a legal matter."

Through his actions, Barack breached the boundaries that existed between the authorities concerning the separation of powers. Because of this ruling, the IHCJ interfered and invaded the decisions of the Israeli Ministry of the Interior, the Ministry of Religions, the IDF and the Ministry of Defence. These government offices are all now controlled by the IHCJ's dictatorship. Barack, a brilliant scholar of law, has issued several more strategies that have allowed the IHCJ to sustain its tyranny over the other authorities.

Besides the "open door" policy that he created, he ruled that the IHCJ is open to any matter or subject that can be discussed in court, reviewed, and referenced for legal determination.

Barack's third strategy is crucial, and it is essential that anyone who lives in Israel and beyond knows of its existence. This third strategy is called the "Principle of Likelihood." The basis of this principle is that the IHCJ can disqualify any government decision, without exception. This principle has designated a virtual prime minister, defence minister, or foreign minister, etc. Should a prime minister decide on an issue in a way that the IHCJ does not like, it will raise a flag that disqualifies the decision, returning with a virtual "likelihood" decision. The virtual minister—the judge—then becomes the decision maker. How can any free country tolerate such a thing? I cannot imagine a Supreme Court judge disqualifying any prime minster or minister's decision and deciding for them! This is the unheard-of reality that the government of Israel has to endure, sometimes daily.

The last foundation of the rulings by Barack is that the IHCJ has the authority to disqualify laws. This authority is an authority given to the Knesset alone. However, Barack's ruling was accepted, and the IHCJ has already disqualified twenty laws so far. The reason for their disqualifications is primarily because of "human rights issues." This is an umbrella claim. For example, the IHCJ disqualified a taxation law for those who purchased and owned three apartments or more. What has that disqualification to do with "human rights"?

By using these four foundations, the IHCJ has developed its leverage over the authorities, who were elected by the people, dictating the destiny of the beautiful nation of Israel.

Sadly, I do not predict that there will be any change soon to fight this enemy within. The current prime minister, Netanyahu, has learned to endure the IHCJ without confronting it. Hopefully, a person with the enthusiasm to represent the people will rise to restore the IHCJ to its place. This will not be an effortless task, and this person will need to be unique and accepted by the majority if they are to bring truly balanced governing back to the land.

Living among my people, I have realized that, for a weird reason, most will not deal with an escalating issue. The reason? "It could get worse." To understand how inadequate this answer is, I need to share a childhood story with you. When I was growing up in Israel, the Palestine Liberation Organization (PLO), a terrorist organization, killed many Israelis by kidnapping and executing travelers on the bus. It was terrible to see the news and see the victims' images, most of whom were very young. One of my uncles mentioned that the Israelis knew where Yasser Arafat was, but they did not want to kill him. Arafat, the terrorist, was the leader of the PLO back in those days.

When I heard my uncle's words, I asked him, "Why will not we kill him? Look how many of us he killed by sending terrorists here!"

My uncle quickly replied, like it was an automatic answer. "Because," he said in heavy tones, "someone worse will come after him."

That was his answer, which I could not accept. "So, we will kill the ones that follow, until they learn their lesson," I replied.

At that comment of mine, my uncle smiled and did not respond.

From a very young age, I have often heard the same answer, in different forms: "It could be worse," "It will not change the reality," etc. I have realized that my people are influential people and people with the ability to endure suffering; they are willing to endure the suffering piled on them, without fighting for change. Sadly, that pattern of behavior has turned against my people several times in history. When the Nazis came to power, the people did not respond as they should, because they claimed "it could be worse" if they resisted. When they realized that the worst was happening, it was too late, and millions were already dead.

The people in Israel have to shake themselves awake and realize that freedom is not free. For 2,000 years, they have suffered tyranny during their time in exile; thus, they have the full right to enjoy liberty in their own nation. This kind of tyranny is quite crafty, since the ideas sound noble when they are propounded in the name of human rights. Most people do not have a complete understanding of the separation-of-power concept and its importance. However, with the proper knowledge, they will hopefully take it to heart and change. To restore the IHCJ to its original position and function, the solutions must be the responsibility of the people who have been chosen.

There are two primary and essential steps to doing so:

1. Enact a fundamental law of the separation of powers, following the examples and conclusions seen in other countries with such patterns, like the US. That foundational law will need to explain how the courts' authorities precisely and specifically fall under the control of the Supreme Court.

2. Nullify all the decisions, strategies, and rulings made by the IHCJ since the 1980s. The best healing process for justice would be for

the people to demand that the Knesset re-appoint a constitution committee. The Knesset majority will select the right professional for the task: someone honorable, with a good name.

Israel needs to have a constitution, for several reasons. The first reason is to protect the rights of the citizens in the land, Jew and non-Jew alike. Second, the constitution will defend democracy and keep the separation of powers in balance. It is about time that the people rise above themselves and fight for the freedom that they truly deserve.

Each nation or group of people has its awakening, a triggering event that causes history to unfold. It was the Boston Tea Party for the people of the US. For the French, it was overtaking the Bastille fortress. I am not encouraging any violent revolution in any shape or form. The people of Israel, if they want freedom, can do it in their usual resilient way, demonstrating peace and electing the right people to make this necessary change. Maybe this chapter will reach the hearts of the right people, causing them to bring freedom to those who dwell in Zion for the sake of generations to come.

The following chapter will focus on Israel's unique confrontation with a specific Jewish community in the world: the American Jewish community. Not all the American Jewish community is at fault; however, some elements within it cannot be ignored, and it is these that turn much of the community against Israel itself.

Chapter 8
THE FEW AFFECTING THE MANY

This chapter is not an easy one for me to write, personally, due to several aspects. The first aspect is that this is the only chapter that focuses on an Israeli opponent who is not living in Israel, being an exception to all the other communities, groups, institutions, and individuals mentioned in this book. The second aspect is that this community is part of my spiritual experience, especially in terms of sharing the good news. They are part of the Jewish people, even though they are not living in Israel.

The community focused on in this chapter is the Jewish community in the United States (US). Now, before someone positions themselves to criticize me or tries to jump down my throat, please continue reading and hold your final decision until the end of this chapter.

First, it is imperative to mention the extraordinary contribution this unique community has made, not just to Israel, but to all humanity. This community has had a glorious past, dating back to the foundation of this American nation. Even the US dollar bill stood as silent evidence of the Jewish community's contribution to the US people's fight for their independence. If you look at a one-dollar bill, you will notice an arrangement of thirteen stars shaped like one star, similar to the Star of David. This symbol is located right above the character of the American Eagle. This Star of David was ordered by none other than President George Washington, revealing a remarkable story that is a part of US history. Washington met Haym Solomon, a wealthy Jewish entrepreneur from Philadelphia, Pennsylvania. Solomon had already donated his wealth to support the colonists and help contribute to the revolution's fight for independence against the British. However, his next contribution was crucial, as following the escalation of the war, the colonies were out of monetary resources. The amount needed was $20,000, which is equal to almost £1 million today. Both amounts mentioned are small change to today's US, but back in those days, for a nation at the time of its birth, that amount was overwhelming.

Washington contacted Solomon, who fully volunteered for the holy mission. Understanding the crucial historical time, Solomon did not even stop for a break on the holiest day of the year for the Jewish people, Yom Kippur; this is a very sacred day revered by the Jews worldwide, during which they fast, repent, and pray for God's mercy. In fact, on that holy day, Solomon went from one synagogue to another, imploring the men who were praying there to contribute toward the war effort. By doing so, he raised the amount needed. Solomon's effort gave Washington the ability to launch the ultimate attack and win the war. As a show of gratitude to Solomon and the Jewish people, the Star of David is found on the dollar bill.

The above story is one of many that show the Jews' contribution to US history. Here is a concise list (with a sincere apology for those whose names are not mentioned):

- Biology and medicine: David Baltimore, in 1975, was a Nobel Prize winner for his research on reverse transcriptase. The biochemist Alfred G. Gilman was a Nobel Prize winner in 1994. H. Robert Horvitz, a biologist, was a Nobel Prize winner in 2002.

- Economics: Gary Becker, was a Nobel Prize winner in 1992. Amy Finkelstein became Professor of Economics at the Massachusetts Institution of Technology (MIT). Ben Bernanke is the former Chair of the US Federal Reserve Bank. (The number of Nobel Prizes winners in this specific field is an impressive eight and counting.)

- Mathematicians: Yakov Eliashberg, Charles Fefferman, Michael Freedman, Sergiu Klainerman, Peter Lax, Elias Stein, and Edward Witten.

- Historians: Norman Finkelstein, Robert Fogel, and Howard Zinn.

- Sports: Mark Spitz, an Olympic swimmer who won seven gold medals in the 1972 Munich Summer Olympics. Aly Raisman, an Olympic gymnastics champion. Mike Brown, Jeff Halpern, Eric Nystrom, Mathieu Schneider, and Jason Zucker are all famous names in ice hockey. Jewish sportspeople cover many fields, including boxing, baseball, basketball, American football, golf, and more.

- Entertainment: There is an almost endless list of Jewish actors, musicians, composers, singers, comedians, directors, producers, models, TV and radio presenters, and even circus performers.

Out of this fascinating long list, some names have to be highlighted:
- Leonard Bernstein, a composer and conductor.
- George Gershwin, a composer and songwriter.
- Scarlett Johansson, an actress.
- Harrison Ford, an actor.
- Kirk Douglas, an actor who also honorably served as a soldier in the US Navy.
- Barbara Streisand, an actress and singer.
- Dustin Hoffman, an actor.
- Woody Allen, a writer, director, and actor.
- Steven Spielberg, a director.
- Jerry Seinfeld, a comedian.
- Jerry Lewis, an actor and comedian and a beloved philanthropist.
- Larry King, a TV and radio host.

As mentioned earlier, this is a partial list of American Jewish entertainers that I have selected. Once this book is published, I genuinely hope that those whose names were not mentioned will not call me in the middle of the night to give me a guilt trip for not mentioning them. I am sure that historical research focusing on this community's contributions to global society could fill several books. Israel considers this community an excellent asset for its help, donations, and use of political leverage to grow and be recognized globally.

However, lately, and gradually, there have been some alarming signs of decline that are sadly leading to a hostile reality affecting Israel itself.

How come? Let us start with the first reason, which is to be observed as the number-one reason for the change in this community's position with Israel. The foremost reason is a demographic decline. The reasons for the demographic decline primarily result from low birth rates—as well as mixed marriages—and immigration to the land of Israel. For several reasons, the number of Jews living in the US is unknown, as the state and religion are separated in the US, and as such, the state does not register a person, when they are born, according to their faith. There are many debates among the global Jewish community regarding who is Jewish and who is not. However, some people consider themselves Jews even if they do not carry the bloodline, just because they wish to be part of the Jewish community and people.

There has been a decline in the Jewish population in the US since 1960. This is an important fact to mention, because demography influences politics. When the Jewish community in the US was at its peak, President Roosevelt issued several civil rights executive orders to protect minorities in the country. The Jews received this status, especially given the fact that they had just endured the Holocaust. The Jewish community, excited to be protected, has voted practically automatically for the Democrat Party since the time of Roosevelt.

However, following the decline in their numbers, the Democrats have shifted to the other minority power rising in the USA: the Muslim immigrants. When Islamic congressional representative Ilhan Omar's made anti-Semite remarks, the Democrat Party did not support the ensuing condemnation. Nancy Pelosi claimed that Omar "did not understand the weight of her words," instead of using more harsh condemnation as might be expected from the House Chair. This kind of political pattern has proven that the Democrat Party is shifting, looking for a more powerful group of voters, the Muslims, whose numbers are rising. Many Jews feel left behind by the Democrat Party, which they have considered their shield and protection for many years.

It would be natural for a community of voters to pursue the conservative side of the map, but reality shows that the voting map does not change radically. Why is this? The answer is the progressives within the Jewish community.

It is necessary to look at the political history of the Jewish community in the US to understand the picture. In the early years of Jews immigrating to the US, back in the 1880s, most of the Jews immigrating had a very conservative point of view. Later, however, reformations within the Jewish communities in Europe, like the enlightenment movement, socialist and communist ideals, and even anarchists, flooded the US with such a massive immigration that the conservative Jews became a small minority. The *Bund*, mentioned earlier in this book, brought many Jewish leaders into the "American Labor Movement," where they helped to find unions and played significant roles in left-wing politics.

The Jewish community, as a persecuted community in Europe and other nations, including Latin America, has stormed America in their fight for human rights—not only their own, but the rights of all minorities. The list of activists who were and are involved in human rights activism is long-probably even challenging the length of the list of American Jewish entertainers. The liberal Jews involved were taking part in and promoting social issues such as workers' rights, civil rights, women's rights, gay and lesbian rights, freedom of religion, freedom from religion, and various other progressive causes. Some are listed below:

- Dinah Abrahamson, who was born in 1954 and died in 2013, was a politician and an activist for the African-Americans in the *Lubavitch* community.
- Gloria Allred is a lawyer and a radio talk show host.
- Maximilian Cohen was an American Socialist Party Leader.
- Ada Fisher is a physician and a perennial issues candidate.
- Rashida Leah Jones is an actress, director, writer, and peace activist.
- Michael Signer is an attorney and a politician.

The list is long and impressive. All of those mentioned in this condensed list are prominent leaders that are fully dedicated to their cause. Their human rights activities are not just limited to the US, but appear globally.

However, most progressives turn a cold shoulder to Israel, mainly because of the Israeli-Palestinian conflict. They ignore the fact that Israel needs to protect itself, surviving in a tough neighborhood called the Middle East, and blame Israel for oppressing people by force. These accusations are as far from the absolute truth as the east is from the west, but they hold their ground, primarily while supported by the US left-wing media.

In this book, I have no will or desire to deal with the Israeli conflict with the invented people called "the Palestinians" (which, in Hebrew means invaders or intruders). I will only offer some defensive remarks about the conflict. There is a peace process in place; meanwhile, Israel suffers ongoing terrorism from the other side, doing its best to defend itself.

Without getting into the details of this unresolved conflict, the bottom line is obvious. Israel's right to defend itself and take steps to protect its people is translated by the human rights activists, the progressives, and the Jews who are activists in such a way that has caused severe damage to Israel's image across the world. They compare Israel to dark regimes like the past apartheid regime in South Africa. They are anti-Zionist, causing many to turn a cold shoulder toward Israel's efforts to survive and defend its people.

Dr. Guy Bechor, an Israeli Middle East analyst, commented in one of the Israeli TV interviews that the American Jewish progressives are considered an enemy that is more dangerous to Israel than the Islamic Republic of Iran. Is there any exaggeration in this statement? Let us examine the facts ourselves. In 2018, Israel had to deal with new terrorism and intimidation from the Gaza strip. The terrorist organization Hamas launched massive attacks on the borders shared with Israel, using their civilians to charge the fenced perimeter, trying to break into Israeli territory. This was not a peaceful demonstration since, during the assault, the mob threw explosive devices, Molotov cocktails, and stones toward the Israeli Defence Force (IDF) soldiers. During these riots, the Hamas terrorists launched rockets and missiles at Israel. In addition, they tried to use several of the tunnels dug underneath the Israeli border to surprise-attack Israeli soldiers or even Israeli civilians.

While Israel was dealing with that challenge, the Jewish progressives organized riots in several cities and universities in the US. They formed anti-Israeli riots, exhibited pictures falsely claiming that Israel was performing genocide, and recited the *Kaddish* (the morning Jewish prayer) for the rioters and the mob who died during their violent acts. At that point, it did not matter whether their claim was the truth. As a result, the media has shown Jewish people graphically standing against those of their people living in the land of Israel.

The truth is this: if any other nation was challenged to protect its borders from rioters and terrorists, as Israel has been, the number of casualties would have been much higher. The Israeli soldiers were given specific orders about when and when not to open fire. There were some cases where the mob's attacks wounded Israeli soldiers before they had even opened fire. However, to the progressives, these facts were not convincing. The progressive Jewish activists would not change their minds. The reason they would not back down is because of their universalist point of view. National values like borders, languages, and flags contradict universalism, according to which national values are outdated and need to be changed. For example, Brexit, Britain's separation from the European Union, was simply a nightmare. Many of the UK citizens could not believe it had happened.

Furthermore, they saw the US as the last frontier, since most European nations were prompting their leaders to adopt nationalism and impose borders and language requirements again. Since they are more vocal than the silent majority, they use the mainstream media to advertise their brainwashing attempts. They push toward defining nationalism as racist, so Israel's act of protecting its borders from invasion is seen as a racial act. These opinions are also accurate regarding the act of stopping illegal immigrants from trying to cross US borders. Protecting a barrier, in their view, is a racist act as well. They also believe that whoever does not think as they do is automatically a racist and a fascist.

However, these progressive Jews completely contradict themselves. By opposing Israel's border policy, they support a fanatical terrorist group like Hamas, whose goal is to become a nation by itself, with a flag! Can you see that contradiction? It is an absurd approach.

Many feminist Jewish American women have wholly embraced the Palestinian people's side, turning a cold shoulder to Israel. They have chosen Linda Sarsour, a devout Muslim woman, to become one of the prominent leaders of the feminist movement. Well, Sarsour is a complete advocate of sharia law. Advocating for such laws contradicts the whole idea of the feminist movement. It calls for unity without any differences in gender, race, and religion while preferring a group of people through a set of laws that are based on religion, race, and gender, elevating the male to oppress the female.

Bernie Sanders, an American Jewish politician, portrays himself as a socialist while being a communist. He ran for presidential office through the Democrat Party primaries and lost. He has frequently verbally attacked Israel; these attacks were so harsh that even the progressives washed their hands of him. During the candidate debates, referring to Prime Minister Netanyahu, he said, "Right now, sadly, tragically, Israel has a reactionary racist now running the country."

Sanders, a person who worked in a kibbutz and lived in Israel back in the 1960s, has said that, if elected President of the US, he would consider taking the US embassy out of Jerusalem and returning it to Tel Aviv. It is an unheard-of remark from a person of Jewish descent, who knows that Jerusalem has a history of 3,000 years in the lives of the Jewish nation. Sanders called the American Israel Public Affairs Committee (AIPAC) a "platform of bigotry," as well as suggesting cutting foreign aid to Israel and redirecting it to the Palestinians instead. Furthermore, he embraces supporters who have called for Israel to be boycotted by organizations such as Boycott, Divestment, Sanctions (BDS), which supports the Palestinians' movement. No wonder President Donald Trump named Sanders "Crazy Bernie."

However, this unreasonable man and many others are causing much damage to Israel's image across the world. They are supporting the enemies of Israel and encouraging anti-Semitism, especially in the US. These very vocal movements and individuals are silencing the minority of conservative Jewish opinions in the American Jewish Community. Sadly, the damage is done, and most of the American Jewish Community does not support Israel as they should.

Here is proof. I was looking at the support of the Jewish Americans, who elected and reelected President Barack Hussein Obama. In 2008, with the winds of change brought by Obama, 77% of the voting American Jews elected Obama president. Four years later, after indicating that President Obama had a clear anti-Israeli policy, there was a drop of only 8%. Thus, 69% of the American Jewish voters still supported Obama, even though he acted negatively toward Israel. This example is vital proof that most of the Jewish community in the US is not in solidarity with Israel, which they should be as they are part of the Jewish nation.

There was a time when American Jews stood with Israel, especially during challenges like wars in the region. These days are, sadly, gone. Many American Jews have declared their support for Israel, but the vocal minority within the community causes the impression among non-Jews that most of the community opposes Israel.

Another aspect that needs to be added to the conflict is the outcome of the 2016 US elections. The elected president for 2016, Trump, was selected with the support of only 30% of the votes from the Jewish community; all the rest supported Hillary Clinton. During the stormy 2016 campaign, Trump was accused of being a racist. He responded by demonstrating that he has Jews employed in his company, that his daughter is a convert to Judaism and that her husband is Jewish. However, this did not change the majority's mindset.

The vocal progressives within the community, helped by influential people involved in the media, in entertainment, and in community leadership, directed the rest of the community to vote for a party that, most of the time, has turned its back on Israel. As a person who lives in the US and does his best to be part of this community, even though rejected following my faith in Yeshua, most Jewish progressives have opposed Trump. This pattern of opposition has remained at the same level, even though Trump has shown significant favor to Israel. Trump recognized Jerusalem as the capital of Israel by moving the US embassy there. To be more accurate, US Congress had already approved moving the embassy to Jerusalem over twenty years ago; however, the Presidents-elect have had the right to postpone the move, out of political favor or for any other reason. In Trump's case, he had promised his voters (who were not only Jewish voters but also evangelical voters supporting that recognition) that he would do so, and he fulfilled that promise.

Trump also recognized the sovereignty of the State of Israel over the Golan Heights. The Golan Heights, a territory taken from the Syrians after an escalation in that area back in the 1960s, has extremely strategic importance to Israel. Unlike previous US presidents, Trump gave the green light to the State of Israel and granted recognition of their sovereignty.

He also stopped the funding of the United Nations Relief and Works Agency (UNRWA), which aid is designated as only being for the Palestinians. Here, these organizations and the UN showed unfairness toward Israel. Trump saw the true colors of reality and decided, rightfully, to defund this organization. Even though during Trump's presidency, the USA and Israel had an excellent relationship, most American Jews would not support Trump as president and even opposed some, or even all, of his policies. There are progressive organizations that even oppose the opinion of most of Israel's public on vital issues. For example, nine Jewish liberal organizations in the US sent a letter to President Trump, pleading to him to keep the "two-state solution."

The two-state solution, which is a failing plan to resolve peace and end the Israeli–Palestinian conflict, urges Israel to retreat from most of the Judah and Samaria areas, destroy the existing Israeli settlements, and divide the capital of Israel, Jerusalem. Naturally, most of Israel's public will not agree to this agreement, and do not believe that the Palestinians are true partners for peace. However, the opinion of most Israelis, in the eyes of these progressive organizations, does not matter. This is further proof of how serious this enemy is to Israel, as it is doing its best to destroy Israel's image internationally and trying to reshape Israel's policy, even while not living in Israel! By this group's actions, it wants to show what is best for Israel; however, doing so is the Israeli people's right, since they live there.

These organizations also give legitimacy to anti-Zionists and anti-Israeli forces active in America, allowing them to continue their agenda against Israel and attempt to change US public opinion of Israel. They are trying to reshape the US citizen's view, mainly by convincing them to remove US aid from Israel. This aid is crucial for Israel's security. If stopped, Israel will be in a dangerous place when confronting its enemies. By continuing their activities, the progressive liberal Jewish movements have indirectly damaged Israel's security.

In summation, the American Jewish population either goes against Israel's policies or, in the best case, remains quiet and non-responsive in the face of vocal liberals and progressives. It is the only Jewish community in the entire world that does not support the conservatives' points of view. For example, 80% of British Jews vote for conservatives and stand behind

Israel. Other Jewish communities, like those in Latin America, also have conservative majorities. Keeping Jerusalem in their minds and hearts was one of the most crucial means by which the Jews survived the diaspora. Furthermore, the Jewish people, by reading the Holy Scriptures, have had a strong desire to restore themselves to the Promised Land, as promised to them by G-d.

Sadly, the Jews in the US, in particular, care more for the LGBTQ community and abortions than in showing concern for Israel. The Jewish people that do not care for Israel do not care for their identity as Jews. Not caring about being Jewish will eventually lead to their disappearance among the nations. They are not as invisible as they think. For now, the only solution for them is to immigrate to Israel. Such an immigration will bring tremendous blessings to Israel, which will receive educated, resilient, and resourceful people who will safely maintain the Jewish identity for their children, grandchildren, and generations to come.

PREFACE TO CHAPTER 9

Several Updates to Events to Be Mentioned Before the Final Chapter

It is Wednesday, December 23, 2020. As I am about to begin reviewing the final chapter of this book, after several meetings with my editor and publisher, I notice news from Israel and the world that it is impossible to ignore. These dramatic news stories, the timings of which are almost parallel, concern the world and the future of Israel, both politically and socially.

Therefore, I have added this preface to the final chapter and have kept that chapter's content as it was initially written.

Let us start with the news from around the world. Following President Donald J. Trump's unprecedented effort and administration, the United States (US) has produced two new vaccines in record time that will apparently end the COVID-19 pandemic. As I write these lines, thousands in the world are taking the vaccines: in the US, Europe, Asia, and even Israel. There are many discussions across the world about the outcome of these efforts, and there is so much to say about this significant event. However, scientists are just learning about the development of the vaccination efforts, so it might take a while to form conclusions and see results.

The parallel dramatic news story is that Israel is going through its fourth election campaign in less than two years. The last coalition formed between the *Likud* Party and the Kachol–Lavan Party survived for less than eight months (this coalition was formed on May 17, 2020). A date for the new election day has not as yet been decided, but I am sure that the need to accommodate COVID-19 regulations will affect the voting rates when it does occur.

The key questions that should now be asked are:

- Will the challenges mentioned in the first chapter of this book grow more significant or more extreme?
- Will these challenges become weaker or ineffective, or will they disappear?

The results of the coming elections campaign will not resolve the considerable challenges nor tackle the enemies within Israel that are mentioned in this book.

Prime Minister Benjamin Netanyahu needs to prepare for an additional major challenge coming from his party. Gideon Sa'ar, a senior member of the *Likud* party and a former education and interior minister, has left the *Likud* Party and challenged Netanyahu by establishing and leading a new party. Following the biblical principle that "A house divided will fall," Netanyahu is confronting one of the biggest challenges of his political career, which probably will end his role as prime minister.

Sadly, the documented and bitter struggle between the two has led to this new outcome. I hope that throughout this campaign, the differences between the two challengers will be discussed and resolved in such a way that leads to the reunion of the *Likud* Party, for Israel's sake.

Sa'ar is one of the greatest and most heroic judges, but his last name means "storm." It is very ironic to realize how his temperament matches his name! Observing this person, I have seen a true warrior and a leader who has caused many storms throughout his career. Sa'ar has stirred up the most significant storm of his lifetime; it remains to be seen whether the outcome of this political hurricane will bring destruction in the future.

Chapter 9
THE FINAL CHAPTER

A few years ago, while sharing the good news with a young Israeli man, I discovered that he was part of an elite special force unit within the Israeli Defence Force (IDF). This veteran told me that, during one of his secret operations in a country that does not share borders with Israel, his team was spotted by the enemy, who responded with fire, causing the death of several of his unit. He and the surviving soldiers carried their dead friends for a few miles in a very hostile area, trying to reach the rescue chopper that would take them from the enemy zone and bring the dead soldiers home to be honorably buried in the land.

The veteran told me that he had PTSD following this event, from which he was set free after he accepted Yeshua as his Lord and Savior. During the funeral of one of his friends, who was lost in the battle, his commander spoke some words of comfort to the families who had lost their dear ones. After doing so, he looked at his soldiers before saying, "The Jewish people are the most sensitive people on earth. They are as sensitive as a cat. Just as a cat is very alert to its environment, so are our people.

"And you," he went on, pointing at the soldiers present, "you are the claws and the teeth of this sensitive nation."

I could do nothing but agree to his commander's words. The Jewish people, having been hated, persecuted, raped, and murdered by other nations for an extended period of time, have developed a unique sensitivity that cannot be compared to any other group of people in the world. Honestly, I cannot think of any nation that could compete with the Jews in terms of the number of atrocities, deaths, and troubles they have experienced. Indeed, after reading my book, I believe that you, my readers will agree with this declaration.

However, resiliency and patience through suffering are two of this nation's qualities, of which I am proudly a member. Through their characters and their sensitivity, the Jewish people have achieved significant victories against their enemies; not just when the Jews went back to the land, but when they were fighting and rebelling against the Nazis, and showing heroism in concentration camps and ghettos, such as that seen in the Warsaw Ghetto Uprising. Unfortunately, however, these actions might be considered to be too late, and taken only by a few people that did not want to be led like sheep to the slaughter. Even so, they are still recognized as acts of heroism.

Jewish heroism, courage, and striking out at the enemy in very sophisticated ways: there are already piles of books written on this very subject. Just one example of the security forces' sophistication can be found in how they eliminated the terrorist Yahya Abd-Al-Latif Ayyash. Ayyash was the chief bomb maker in the terrorist organization Hamas, who orchestrated the death of over 100 Israeli civilians by making strap bombs, strapping them to suicide terrorists, and sending these men to detonate themselves on Israeli buses full of passengers. He was active from 1992 until his assassination in 1996.

The Israeli General Security Service (GSS) and the IDF so wanted Ayyash that every soldier carried his picture as a way to help with his capture. Ayyash was in hiding, running from one secret location to another, using the help of others within Hamas. The way he was assassinated is very unusual. Using sophisticated methods and espionage, the GSS delivered a cellphone to Yahya, which he and his helper presumed was his phone. This phone, however, had a small C4 explosive planted in it.

Even today, intelligence agencies have not managed to figure out how the Israelis deceived the enemy and delivered an assassination tool to this murderer. Once Ayyash received the phone, he received a phone call—his last one. The number appearing on it seemed to be the phone number of one of his relatives, calling to ask him how he was doing. Yahya picked up the call and put the cellphone next to his ear, saying *"Naam"* ("Hello" in Arabic). On the other end of the line, someone asked, "Yahya?", to which he replied with another "Naam."

That would be the last word this mass murderer said on this earth before being sent to hell for eternity. On the other end of the line, a sophisticated audio identification machine confirmed the terrorist's voice and a finger pushed a button to detonate the explosive inside the cellphone. The explosion severed Ayyash's head from his body. Those who heard the explosion entered the terrorist's hiding place, then realised that there was nothing for them to do but start preparing for his funeral.

The main reason for sharing this story is to show the sensitivity of the people in Israel. The GSS knew for a while where this terrorist was hiding, and could have launched a missile straight at the apartment, as they had done with other terrorists. They could have sent a special forces unit to eliminate him. However, sensitivity prevailed. This specific person killed more than a hundred Israelis by designing bombs, so the most brilliant minds built a bomb intended for this murderer.

The Jewish people are sensitive people, sometimes overly sensitive, but they have claws, and these claws are sharp. The Israelis have learned how to deal with our external enemies. Whether they are near to or far from Israel, those who do evil to Israel, or who pose a threat to the land and its people, are destroyed or rendered incapable of harming Israel. This has created a tremendous deterrence effect. Examples of this pattern whereby Israel deals with its enemies include both large-scale and pinpoint operations. However, any such list has to start with a brilliant process that Israel conducted in 1967: the six-day war.

Are you aware that the most prestigious military academy, West Point, does not teach about the Six-Day War? At West Point, they consider this war (which was started as an operation) to be an Act of God. Some have even declared that there was a hidden hand throughout the war, that it was a miracle. This war was not supposed to be called the "six-day" war, it was supposed to be called the "two-hour" war, after Israel destroyed the entire Egyptian air force. After that strike, Israel completed all the rest of its missions in a domino effect; the highlight of this achievement was Israel's conquering of the city of Jerusalem, following which they took control of the Temple Mount. Once again, after 2,000 years, the Jews gained the right to worship freely in Jerusalem and pray by the Western Wall.

Another expert operation is the Mossad Operation that followed the Munich Massacre. The Palestinian terrorist organization "Black September" took advantage of the weak security during the 20th Olympic Games that took place in Munich, Germany, to attack the Israeli athletes, take them hostage, and eventually murder eleven of them. This news was devastating in Israel. That Israelis were murdered in Germany affected the Israelis greatly, evoking horrific memories of the Holocaust in Nazi Germany. Because of these sad events, the Israeli Mossad took responsibility by dismissing two of the officials who had failed to secure the athletes even though they had received earlier intel about a terrorist attack on Israeli targets. Mossad also offered Prime Minister Golda Meir a way to assassinate those who had planned, provided training for, and funded the terrorist attack.

The Israeli Mossad agents assassinated several of those responsible for the Munich Massacre, located throughout Europe and in other countries. Eventually, they eliminated the "Red Prince," Ali Hassan Salameh, the terrorist who had designed and orchestrated the Munich Massacre. He was the chief commander of "Black September," the armed force of the terrorist Palestine Liberation Organization (PLO). Killing him was difficult since international intelligence agencies protected Salameh for their own reasons. Mossad trained a unique unit for this high-priority task, one member of which was a woman. This woman was the one who pushed the explosives. The remote-controlled button was pressed precisely at the moment that Salameh's vehicle passed by a parked-up vehicle full of explosives. As a result, Salameh and his four bodyguards were eliminated.

I have mentioned these operations and missions to emphasize a reality about my people. The fact is, the Jewish people have a sensitive nature. Israel reacts personally to a brutal killing of any Israeli or Jewish man or woman in the world that is the result of animosity, hatred, or anti-Semitism. Sensitivity is an excellent quality that the Jews use to deal with their vicious external enemies. However, that same sensitivity does not work when dealing with the enemies within. Israel protects those who dwell in Zion; it still does not know how to deal with those who destroy Israel through their actions and from the inside.

As a democracy that supports freedom of speech, journalism, and religion, Israel will allow even the most hateful speeches against Israel, even addresses that call for the destruction of Israel. Since the beginning of modern Israel's existence, no speaker, of any opinion, has been arrested for sharing their thoughts publicly. If they were arrested or asked to answer questions by the security forces, this is usually the result of a violent event that followed their speech. This pattern of behavior proves, again and again, the sensitivity of the Jewish people regarding people's freedom, expressions, and respect for the dignity and holiness of life.

As an Israeli who believes in Yeshua, I have been asked the following question many times: "How can we pray for Israel?" It is this question that has led me to write this book. I believe, with all my heart, that the enemies within Israel could cause Israel to be destroyed from within (Heaven forbid). Therefore, this book offers so many ways for you, dear reader, to pray for Israel. For years, Christian believers have been instructed to pray for Israel's protection from its outside enemies; however, these prayers have neglected the enemies within. The complexity of dealing with these internal enemies is so vast that the only solution is prayer; that is, they must be dealt with through faith alone. It would be too far-fetched to think that we might find a solution or solutions to deal with the current situation. Only the God of Israel, the same God that took his people out of Egypt, can deal with the land's current internal enemies. Only He can and will restore the hearts of many, causing them to repent and turn their hearts toward Him and bless His people in the land given to them.

The Bible is full of descriptions of Israel's restoration and of becoming a blessing to itself and the surrounding nations. For example, in Isaiah 6, it is written "Arise, shine, for your light has come, and the glory of the Lord has risen upon you" (Isaiah 6:1). The prophet here offers an end-time prophecy that not only describes Israel's restoration but sets Israel as an example, a model for all the nations. This prophecy has not yet been fulfilled, but it will be fulfilled at the Messiah's second coming. It is clear from this verse that major spiritual warfare will occur before the miraculous shining on God's people. Indeed, while darkness both outside and inside the land of Israel will rise to destroy Israel. a supernatural event will occur that will bring peace, world repentance, prosperity, and righteousness.

This chapter brings much comfort through the realization that all the enemies of Israel, wherever they are, will be eliminated for eternity. At first, I thought of offering some solutions of how to deal with Israel's enemies within. However, once I was exposed to the multitude of enemies and the complexity of steps that needed to be taken to overcome them, I concluded that any overcoming by Israel has to be supernatural.

When Israel won the Six-Day War, the people declared, "All glory to the IDF!" Such a disappointing statement to be announced by the people who suddenly gained control over Jerusalem after 2,000 years. The people should have glorified the God of Israel, who had given His people the strength to be victorious. Instead, the people were too proud, biased, and unaware of the supernatural interventions that had occurred during the Six-Day War.

Neither did the people give thanks to Him for bringing back people from the ashes of the Holocaust of Nazi Europe; these people came back to their land, survived several wars, then won a brilliant victory in 1967. In Deuteronomy 8, Moshe (Moses) warned the people of Israel not to be boastful when gaining victory over their enemies. Once the people had said, "All glory to the IDF," they had boastfully declared in their hearts, "My power and the strength of my hand brought me this wealth" (Deuteronomy 8:17). By doing so, they have broken God's commandment by not giving glory to the God of Israel.

The fundamental problem for Israel when dealing with its enemies is Israel itself. Instead of following the examples of its godly ancestors (such as

Joshua, the judges, and kings such as King David from the Bible), Israel uses politics, world knowledge, and, often, numbness to deal with its enemies. The Bible declares that Israel will be restored once it returns to the land after an exile of many years.

Years ago, my Bible college professor said, "If you are dealing with a problem too big to handle, just break it and resolve the broken parts, until naturally, the issue resolves itself." If we know more details about Israel's internal problems, we can pray separately for answers to specific problem; this might bring victory to Israel and glory to our God. From my own experience and involvement with my dear brothers and sisters in the Messiah's body, I know that many are praying for Israel. Some of them even fast for Israel's salvation and even for Israel's enemies, which is a good direction of prayer.

I want to urge and encourage those who pray to focus their prayers on the matters mentioned in this book; in this way, they can bring healing to the Land of Israel, preparing Israel for their forthcoming redemption, which will surely come through Yeshua the Messiah. Please cherish in your heart this verse from Isaiah: "For Zion's sake I will not keep silent, and for Jerusalem's sake, I will not keep quiet, until her righteousness goes forth like brightness and her salvation like a torch that is burning" (Isaiah 62:1).

This verse was and still is my encouraging verse; I use it to pray for my people and share the good news with them. May this verse be your guide when praying and thinking about Israel! The outcome will be rewarding to Israel, the nations, and all the families of the earth who choose the God of Israel as their God. You and your family will be there to celebrate a victorious Israel with Him on a glorious day. Amen.

For author interviews or more information contact:

Shaul Katzav
C/O Advantage Books
info@advbooks.com

To purchase additional copies of these books, visit our bookstore at
www.advbookstore.com

Orlando, Florida, USA
"we bring dreams to life"™
www.advbookstore.com

www.ingramcontent.com/pod-product-compliance
Lightning Source LLC
LaVergne TN
LVHW020059090426
835510LV00040B/2513